Theory/Theatre

Theory/Theatre provides a unique and engaging introduction to literary theory as it relates to theatre and performance. Mark Fortier lucidly examines current theoretical approaches, from semiotics, poststructuralism, through cultural materialism, postcolonial studies and feminist theories.

Drawing upon examples from Shakespeare through Aphra Behn, to Chekhov, Artaud, Cixous and Churchill, the author examines the specific realities of theatre in order to come to a richer understanding of the relations between performance and cultural theory.

Theory/Theatre is the only study of its kind and will be invaluable reading for beginning students and scholars of performance studies.

Mark Fortier is Associate Professor of English at the University of Winnipeg. He has published on Shakespeare, contemporary theatre, cultural studies and theory.

Theory/Theatre

An Introduction

Mark Fortier

LONDON AND NEW YORK

First published 1997
by Routledge
11 New Fetter Lane, London EC4P 4EE

Simultaneously published in the USA and Canada
by Routledge
29 West 35th Street, New York, NY 10001

© 1997 Mark Fortier

Typeset in Palatino by Keystroke, Jacaranda Lodge, Wolverhampton
Printed and bound in Great Britain by Clays Ltd, St Ives plc

British Library Cataloguing in Publication Data
A catalogue record for this book is available from the British Library

Library of Congress Cataloging in Publication Data
A catalogue record for this book has been requested

ISBN 0–415–16164–9 (hbk)
ISBN 0–415–16165–7 (pbk)

Contents

ACKNOWLEDGEMENTS

I owe a great deal to a completely gratuitous act of generosity on the part of Herbert Blau in the early stages of this project. Talia Rodgers at Routledge guided my work from its inception – my title is a variation on one suggested by her. My basic understanding of theatre I learned from Skip Shand, who has given me years of encouragement. Linda Hutcheon showed much appreciated enthusiasm for an early draft of part of this book. The anonymous readers for Routledge have helped make my book much better than it would otherwise have been. Research was done mainly at the University of Toronto and at theatres in Toronto, Peterborough and Stratford, Ontario, and in New York and London. The University of Winnipeg kindly provided a discretionary grant to help pay the costs of the index, which was prepared by Elizabeth Hulse. I would like to thank my friends at Scarabeus Theatre, Daniela Essart and Søren Nielsen, for permission to use their photograph for the cover of this book. Faye Pickrem held my hand and gave me counsel through the long process. Finally, I dedicate this book to my parents, Charles and Gloria Fortier, whose unconditional love and support have helped me through life's rough spots.

INTRODUCTION

There are more things in heaven and earth, Horatio,
Than are dreamt of in your philosophy.[1]

For questioning is the piety of thought.[2]

WHY THIS BOOK?

1

We are fast approaching the end of a millennium, with suitably
dire or utopian speculations on what the new age will be like:
images of angels, cyberspace and global disaster weave their
way through our cultural revery. What is less often remarked
upon in such a momentous situation is that we are also fast
approaching the end of a century, a century of great wars,
technocracy and human mobility, among other things. What is
even less frequently noted is that we are approaching the end
of a half century or less of intense activity in the area of cultural
theory.

Cultural theory, of course, began at least as far back as

ancient Greece. Our own theoretical era, broadly conceived, began in the nineteenth century with G.W.F. Hegel, Karl Marx and Friedrich Nietzsche, continued into the early twentieth century with Sigmund Freud and Ferdinand de Saussure, and then into the middle of this century with, among others, Mikhail Bakhtin, Antonio Gramsci, Walter Benjamin and Simone de Beauvoir. But it is really since the 1960s that cultural theory, or just plain 'theory' as we now call it, has become a ubiquitous and dominant force in academic and cultural environments. Deconstruction, feminism, post-colonialism, semiotics, queer theory, postmodernism, and so forth, have come to define for many the most fruitful and appropriate ways of looking at culture, politics and society. Somewhat like Latin in the Middle Ages and early Renaissance, theory has become the *lingua franca* which allows people in many nations and in such widely disparate fields as literature, history, sociology, architecture and law to find a common ground and vocabulary for their discussions.

Theatre is another area in which theory has had a powerful influence. There are learned journals rife with theoretical studies of theatre and many books which apply deconstruction, semiotics, psychoanalysis or some other theoretical perspective to various theatrical works. There is not so far, however, a book which sets out to introduce the theatre student to a broad range of theory at a basic or intermediate level. In the simplest and most obvious sense, this book is intended to be such an introduction. The primary meaning of its title points in this direction: for the student who simply wants to know more about theory's possible relevance to theatre, this book is a systematic introduction of the application of theory to theatre.

All disciplines where theory has encroached have offered a degree of resistance: for some, theory is too abstruse, too jargon-ridden, too divorced from practicality. In theatre studies especially, theory has not had the open-armed acceptance that

Latin had as the *lingua franca* of an earlier era. Theory has often seemed too contemplative an activity to be more help than hindrance in such a practical pursuit as theatre. Theatre is not made in the mind or on the page. Moreover, much of the theory discussed in this book is often referred to, at least in literature departments, as 'literary theory'. Why should this be so? After all, this theory comes from a broad range of disciplines: philosophy, linguistics, psychoanalysis, political economy, history, anthropology and so forth. To call these theories literary theory is in large part a misrecognition. It is, however, a misrecognition which reveals something about a great deal of theory.

Much of the theory under discussion – not all of it, certainly, but enough to indicate a degree of hegemony – stresses the importance of language as the basis, even the fate, of human activity. For instance, Saussure, in proposing a general theory of signs, argues that linguistic signs will serve as the master-pattern for all others; Jacques Lacan, bringing this linguistic emphasis to psychoanalysis, argues that the unconscious is structured like a language and the subject is a chain of signifiers; Jacques Derrida, positing an 'arche-writing' which underlies language, words and speech, proposes a 'grammatology' or science of writing which would dominate even linguistics.[3]

Theories which are profoundly caught up in questions of language and writing have been more easily, more systematically and more fully applied to literature and other forms of writing than to art forms and cultural practices which emphasize the non-verbal. It becomes easy to think that activities involving writing are somehow at the heart of being human. Theorists of literature have appropriated language-based theories from other disciplines to such an extent that for many working in theory and literature all theory has become in effect literary theory. So it is designated, for instance, in the recent encyclopedias of Irena Makaryk and Michael Groden and Martin Kreisworth.[4]

What happens to more or less non-verbal activities in the face of this emphasis on language and writing? Can literary theory do them justice? Many involved in theatre have been suspicious of this verbal hegemony in recent theory. To treat everything as language or as dominated by language seems a distortion of the nature of theatre as rooted in the physical, the sensual and the visceral as much as it is in the verbal and ideational.

Those who study theatre make a commonplace distinction between drama and theatre. Drama is most often written language, the words ascribed to the characters which in the theatre are spoken by actors. As a written form, drama is easily appropriated by literary theory; it is understandable in the same general terms as fiction, poetry or any other form of letters. The affinity of drama and literature has produced a tendency for literary theory and literary studies to think of theatrical activity as drama rather than as theatre.

Unlike drama, theatre is not words on a page. Theatre is performance, though often the performance of a drama text, and entails not only words but space, actors, props, audience and the complex relations among these elements. Literary theory has often ignored all this. Moreover, if it doesn't reduce theatre to drama, literary theory is capable of making an even bolder gesture in which theatre is brought under the hegemony of language and writing in another way. Here theatre becomes a system of non-verbal signs, non-verbal languages, non-verbal writing, yet dominated still by the hegemony of language and letters as master-patterns for the workings of the non-verbal. Theatre too is a literature. A big question remains: is theatre fully understandable when dominated by a linguistic model?

One side effect of literary theory's domination of theatre is that, despite the assimilation of drama into literary studies and *performance i.e. theatre in its widest context*

despite the attempt to see theatre as non-verbal literature, literary theory ignores those who have made the most profound contributions to a specific theory of theatre: drama and theatre belong to literary theory but theatre theorists do not. For instance, neither of the encyclopedias by Mararyk and Groden and Kreisworth has separate entries for Bertolt Brecht or Antonin Artaud. To anyone involved in theatre theory, these omissions are nothing short of shocking, as much as if Saussure, Freud or Derrida were absent. But shock gives way to speculation: Brecht and Artaud think about theatre in a way that is profoundly different from the way literary theory does, perhaps in a way that literary theory has trouble recognizing.

Given these concerns, to those in theatre with a strong and entrenched antipathy to theory, my book is likely to be – although this is not how I intended it – as much an affront as it is an introduction. In large measure this is unavoidable. Although my purpose is not to shove theory down anyone's throat (to use a Canadian turn of phrase), one of the key insights of much theory is that we cannot control how what we write or say will be taken by others – theatre people know this already in the context of performance. Those who are enthusiastic or open to theory, however, who are curious or merely willing to hold their judgement in temporary abeyance, might see in this book not an attempt to conquer theatre under the flag of theory, but rather an attempt to create a place for dialogue, exploration and questioning. For instance, one of the themes that runs throughout my discussion is the friction between language-based theory and the non-verbal aspects of theatre. For me, the point is not to reject language-based theory but to map the limits of its relevance with care and openness. Similarly, I think the relations between practice and reflection are not susceptible to easy demarcation. The word 'drama' comes from a word related to the Greek verb 'to do'; 'theatre', on the other hand, comes from a word related to the verb 'to see'. Theatre, of necessity, involves both doing and seeing, practice and contemplation. Moreover, the word 'theory' comes from the same root as 'theatre'. Theatre and theory are both contemplative pursuits, although theatre has a practical and sensuous side which contemplation should not be allowed to overwhelm.

This book, therefore, seeks in the engagement of theory and theatre questions to pose to each. Is theatre a kind of language or, if not, how does it escape this master-pattern? If there is something about the theatre which is different from language, how does this reflect on the hegemony of language and writing in theory's understanding of the world? The resistance to theory offered by theatre, or put more benignly, the insistence that theatre have a voice in a true dialogue with theory, points to a second meaning in my title. Theory can be applied to theatre, but in the other direction, theatre speaks back to theory. This is especially so in theatre pieces which themselves enact or induce complex thinking. Much of Shakespeare, for instance, is highly sophisticated reflection on theatre, culture and reality. In this context, the title of this book also invokes such concepts as 'fiction/theory' or 'performance/theory': fictions or performances which are themselves works of theory[5] (as distinct from performance theory or theory of performance widely conceived[6]).

Suspicion about theory has come from other places in theatre studies. Bonnie Maranca, editor of *Performing Arts Journal*, which has been quite open to theoretical work, has recently questioned the use of theory in theatre studies. Although she rejects the separation of practice and production from thinking and reflection, she condemns what she sees as the knee-jerk and formulaic application of theory, a 'dogmatic corruption' of the openness that theory should entail.[7] In an introductory volume, some simplification is necessary. But I have not, I hope, written a dogmatic work. Rather, I would like this to be taken as an 'interrogative text'. I take this idea from Catherine Belsey's *Critical Practice*; according to Belsey, an interrogative text 'invite[s] the reader to produce answers to the questions it implicitly or explicitly raises'.[8] My summary of theories, issues and relations is always incomplete and regularly put forward as a set of explicit or implicit questions rather than a set of conclusions. Theories produce variant and often contradictory ways of looking at issues; I have tried to keep that space of disagreement open. There is nothing definitive about my accounts of theory or my readings of plays; the reader is encouraged to treat them as provisional and revisable. On the largest scale, I am not arguing for any necessary relation between theory and theatre. Readers will work out the relation for themselves. I am not opposed to answers being suggested to the questions I raise, but I prefer a more open-ended interrogation, in which answers never fully arrive. Like Antonin Artaud, I would like 'not to define thoughts but *to cause thinking*'.[9]

2

There is a large body of literature concerned with theories specifically related to the theatre. Bernard F. Dukore's *Dramatic Theory and Criticism: Greeks to Grotowski* is a useful anthology, although it stops somewhat short of the present.[10] Marvin Carlson's *Theories of the Theatre: A Historical and Critical Survey, from the Greeks to the Present*, first published in 1984, expanded in 1993, is a monumental digest which maps to a dizzying degree the range of western theorization about theatre. Theorists not generally associated with the theatre – Freud, Barthes, Derrida, Lyotard – are represented inasmuch as they have occasionally produced essays on theatrical topics.[11]

Dukore and Carlson are not specifically concerned with the relations of theory in general to theatre; however, other writers have taken up aspects of these relations: Mohammad Kowsar has produced essays on Deleuze and Lacan; Gerald Rabkin and Elinor Fuchs have written essays on deconstruction and theatre; Keir Elam's *The Semiotics of Theatre and Drama* is an overview of semiotic analysis related to plays; Sue-Ellen Case, Jill Dolan, and Gayle Austin have each written a book which introduces feminist theories to the study of theatre and drama.[12] These are just a few of the works which take up the application of cultural theory to the theatre.

Most of these works tackle a specific area of concern: deconstruction, semiotics, feminism; there are works, however, which attempt to engage with the broadest possible spectrum of theoretical concerns. No individual has carried such an engagement further than has Herbert Blau who, in a series of complex and difficult books, has taken up ideas from marxism, psychoanalysis, feminism, deconstruction and phenomenology, and from thinkers ranging from Marx and Freud to Benjamin, Lacan, Kristeva, Derrida, Foucault, Deleuze and Baudrillard. All of these theories are sent spinning through Blau's particular perspectives towards a complex and inevitably contradictory metaphysical pessimism. Blau is not for beginners.[13] A different approach is taken by the recent collection *Critical Theory and Performance*, which presents essays by different writers grouped under specific theoretical perspectives: cultural studies; semiotics and deconstruction; marxism; feminism(s); theatre historiography; hermeneutics and phenomenology; psychoanalysis. Each area is given a general introduction, but each section of the collection then proceeds into disparate and very particular applications of theoretical concerns.[14]

Given, then, the extensive work in the fields of theory and theatre, which I can only begin to suggest, what does this book of mine have to offer? As summary, this book – like the recent encyclopedias mentioned earlier – takes advantage of its relative belatedness to look back on a field that has had time to take on a certain shape. As the twentieth century draws to a close, twentieth-century theory begins to seem more set in its patterns than it did ten or twenty years ago. From this vantage I have attempted to grasp theory as broadly constituted. Unlike Carlson or Manfred Pfister,[15] I am specifically concerned with theories that come from outside theatre; unlike Elam and Case, I have attempted to deal with theory as broadly as possible.

As an introduction, this book enters the discourse at a much lower level of complexity than does the work of Herbert Blau. Like Blau, however, and unlike *Critical Theory and Performance*, I speak in a single voice in an attempt to give the field the coherence that such a digestion allows. This is not to say that plurality and multiplicity of voice are not a deeper way of understanding theory, but perhaps plurality and multiplicity are not the best place to start.

WHICH THEORIES? WHICH THEATRE?

This is not just a book about theory; nor is it only about theatre. 'Theory/Theatre' implies a double articulation, which is evident in the structure of the following chapters. I have organized the discussion of theory and the theatre not around schools of theory or the work of particular theorists but rather around issues related to the theatre; theories are discussed inasmuch as they relate to the specific issue under discussion. These issues are grouped under three broad headings. Chapter 1 deals with the relations between the verbal and the non-verbal on the stage, with theatre as text and theatre as embodied, material event. Issues of signification, representation, meaning, understanding, words and silence, the stage, life, body and voice are explored. Chapter 2 deals with the people involved in theatre, with subjectivity, agency, author, character, performer, audience and the collaborations which theatre entails among all those involved. Chapter 3 addresses theatre as an institution in the world and theatre's relations with the world outside the playhouse; here the issues include the historical, economic and political forces which tie theatre in a highly specific way to a particular time and place.

Within each of these chapters, I have chosen to deal with the specific theoretical schools which seem most appropriate to the issue under consideration. Several caveats are in order. First, I have not undertaken an exhaustive discussion of cultural theory, but rather have tried to give a broad, general coverage of those movements that seem most relevant to the study of theatre. Second, I have tailored each school I do discuss to the concerns of a particular chapter, so that each school is presented more narrowly than it would be in a work devoted solely to doing justice to that school. For instance, feminism is dealt with in Chapter 2, on subject and agency. Although much of feminism is about the effect of gender on subjectivity, feminism is also deeply concerned with the subject's relations with the world, and so could have been discussed in Chapter 3. I ask the reader to remember that each school I discuss has a broader range of interest and application than my structure enumerates. Also, I have dealt with individual theorists under the rubric of particular schools of theory. This is less of a distortion for some theorists than for others: Freud is obviously a psychoanalytic thinker. Many theorists, however, have hybrid interests. Gayatri Chakravorty Spivak, discussed here under post-colonialism, combines in her work marxism, deconstruction, feminism and post-colonialism. Julia Kristeva, discussed here under psychoanalytic theory, combines feminism, semiotics and psychoanalysis.

Similar problems of categorization are faced by anyone who attempts to give a systematic arrangement to the field of cultural theory: the editors of *Critical Theory and Performance*, for instance, raise similar fears of arbitrariness and distortion.[16]

For the sake of a necessary expedience and a certain kind of clarity, I have imposed an order on these theories which cannot help but simplify the connections between them.

Given these caveats, the theoretical movements I discuss are arranged in the following order. In Chapter 1, on textuality and embodiment, I discuss semiotics, phenomenology and deconstruction. Among the theorists discussed in this chapter are Ferdinand de Saussure, Charles Peirce, Martin Heidegger, Maurice Merleau-Ponty, Jacques Derrida, and Paul de Man. In Chapter 2, on subjectivity and agency, I discuss psychoanalytic theory, feminist and gender theory, including queer theory, and reader-response and reception theory. Among the theorists covered in Chapter 2 are Sigmund Freud, Jacques Lacan, Julia Kristeva, Virginia Woolf, Judith Fetterley, Jill Dolan, Adrienne Rich, Eve Kosofsky Sedgwick, Wolfgang Iser and Hans Robert Jauss. In Chapter 3, on theatre and the world, I discuss materialist theory, postmodernism and post-colonialism. Among the theorists in this chapter are Louis Althusser, Raymond Williams, Walter Benjamin, Michel Foucault, Fredric Jameson, Linda Hutcheon, Jean Baudrillard, Jean-François Lyotard, Gianni Vattimo, Edward Said, Gayatri Spivak, Trinh T. Minh-Ha, Homi Bhabha and Augusto Boal.

Each chapter, therefore, is divided into three sections, each dealing with a particular theoretical movement. Within each section there is an attempt to give an overview of that movement, a discussion of particular theorists associated with that movement, particular critics who have applied this theory to the study of theatre, and then an exploration of this theory in light of an application to particular works or questions of theatre.

Theory and theatre, as I have noted, can have a number of different relationships. Theatre can sometimes be analogous or equivalent to theoretical reflection; this is how, for example, I position the relationship between phenomenology and Anton

Chekhov, or deconstruction and Artaud or Blau. Closely related – sometimes interchangeable – are cases in which theatre enacts a theoretical position; here, for example, I would point to psychoanalytic theory and Hélène Cixous, feminist theory and Caryl Churchill's *Cloud Nine*, or post-colonialism and the projects of Augusto Boal. Moreover, theory can be used to explain or elucidate theatre in general or particular works of theatre; Derrida on representation and presence is an example of the first, my deconstructive reading of Jerzy Grotowski's *Akropolis* and postmodern reading of Anna Deavere Smith's *Twilight: Los Angeles* examples of the second. Finally, theatre can answer back to theory, calling presuppositions into question and exposing limitations and blindness; the theatrical 'desemiotics' which questions the semiotic rage for finding meaning, the exploration of the way Peter Brook's *Midsummer Night's Dream* takes reader-response theory in complex new directions, or the way Shakespeare's theatre troubles the simpler pieties of materialist analysis are all examples of the confrontation of theory with theatre. Often, of course, several relations are at work at once: Cixous both enacts and questions psychoanalytic theory. The most important point to make about this variety is that it would be fruitless and misleading to try and limit it, especially in an introductory volume which hopes to open up possibilities.

Earlier I drew a distinction between drama, as words on a page, and theatre, as enactment on stage. To this picture it is necessary to add the concept of performance. Performance in a narrow sense refers to certain para-theatrical activities – happenings, demonstrations, museum exhibits involving human participants, and so forth – which are related to theatre in the traditional sense. Performance more widely conceived refers to any performative human activity – everything from murder trials and elections to religious and social rituals, to everyday acts, such as a high school English class or shaving in front of a mirror. Drama, theatre and performance are related activities. One way of thinking of the relationship is to see drama as a part of theatre and theatre as a part of performance. Seeing this relationship points out the difficulty involved in trying to separate a concern with drama from, say, a concern with theatre. To discuss drama is to discuss a part of theatre. Theatre studies are rightly wary that literature studies tend to reduce theatre to drama. This does not mean that theatre studies can study only theatre and not drama. A full study of theatre must be open to words on the page. Moreover, a study of theatre which does not see its relation to performance in general has made an artificial and limiting distinction.

My subject, therefore, is theatre, but this will often entail regard for the drama text and understanding of the place of theatre in a wider field of performance, as well as occasional reference to performance art and performances in everyday life. To stray too far into performance, however, would be to lose focus, while to dwell too much on drama would reduce this study to the narrowly literary. Nevertheless, the reader will note that dramatic elements play a large part in my discussion. This is in part because drama, as fixed and recordable, is the part of theatre most accessible to examination and analysis. Moreover, the drama text remains, especially in the western tradition, a seminal aspect of theatre. Herbert Blau has written, 'I cannot imagine a theatre form of any consequence which does not hold discourse among the modes of meaning.'[17] I would say, rather, that some theatre of consequence has eschewed words and their residue, but more often words are not only one among several modes of meaning, but are given a place of prominence.

The examples I have taken from theatre are guided by a desire to reach a broad, general audience, and by my own expertise and limitations. Consequently, most of my examples are from Europe and the Americas; except for a large dose of Shakespeare, they are predominantly from the twentieth century; many of them are canonical. Within these limitations I have tried to present a broad range of examples, some of which are newer or marginal works which challenge the hegemony of canonical norms. I do not offer this selection as definitive or as a discouragement to other applications.

WHO IS SPEAKING?

One of the foremost insights that feminism, especially, has brought to theory is the need to articulate the position from which one speaks. Who one is (one's experience, biases and investments) is thought to have an inevitable effect on how one reasons. The actual import of such a positioning is open to question. How exactly does any position authenticate, detract from or at least inform one's arguments? How necessary a bond is there between who we are and what we are able to think? At any rate, however, it has become imprudent and naive to ignore the position from which one speaks, and self-declarations have become commonplace in writing that takes feminist theory seriously.

The major difference, for instance, between the first and the expanded edition of Marvin Carlson's *Theories of the Theatre* is that recent feminist theory is given an extended treatment in the newer edition. This treatment leads Carlson to declare his own positionality:

> The materialist recognition that positions of theory, even of identity, are historically and culturally positioned means, as Jill Dolan has argued, that as a theorist she is challenged 'to reposition myself constantly, to keep changing my seat in the theatre, and to continually ask: How does it look from over there?' Such repositioning is perhaps even more of a challenge if one is, like me, culturally positioned on the dominant side of all the traditional discourses – a white, middle-class, academic, heterosexual male.[18]

To position myself in a personal history, I, like Carlson, am a white, heterosexual male. Whatever privilege this affords has been joined with a personal and intellectual history of discomfort with this position. As to class, my life feels like a roller-coaster ride, and employment and financial security has been a long time coming. If simple homologies are at all compelling, one might see this personal history of privilege, uncertainty and disappointment played out in this project as the hubris of the undertaking itself and the questioning and doubt that inform the examination.

One aspect of personal history not covered by Carlson but worth mentioning is nationality. I am a Canadian. From a Canadian perspective, works by Americans or the English often seem blindly to take their Americanness or Englishness for granted. If nationality informs this study, it is in the way I try to leave open and unoccupied any sense of being at a centre which unintentionally marginalizes everyone from somewhere else.

But one has an intellectual as well as a personal history, and often this intellectual history is at least as relevant to how one thinks. Of the theories examined here, I am most invested, on the one hand, in the rigorous suspicion of deconstruction, and on the other in the historical and political insistence of materialist theory; somewhere, somehow, I also retain, especially as someone interested in theatre, an affinity with phenomenology's involvement in bringing the world to light for embodied consciousness. I do not consider myself, however, a deconstructionist or a phenomenologist and, although I do consider myself a materialist, I do not cling to any dogmatic or even orthodox marxism.

Having noted these affinities, I want to stress that I have tried to hold on to a principle of pluralist openness in the following chapters. There is much doubt in recent politicized theory as to whether pluralism and neutrality are possible;

accordingly, sometimes introductory works like this one are written from an openly partisan position: Terry Eagleton's *Literary Theory*[19] or Jill Dolan's *The Feminist Spectator as Critic*, for instance. Such a strategy has its own political and heuristic strengths, including focus and candor. There do, however, seem to be varying degrees of partisanship, and in many aspects of life we expect or hope that, despite their biases, people will attempt to retain some degree of neutrality. And so other works, Sue-Ellen Case's *Feminism and Theatre* or Carlson's *Theories of the Theatre*, for instance, attempt to maintain a more or less open stance. Pluralism has its limits both in its viability and in its usefulness; but it has its strengths too, especially in a work that aims to be interrogative as well as introductory.

Since this is an interrogative work, one important reason for pluralism is to maintain a healthy scepticism and doubt. There are many things, theoretical and political, about which I remain, and perhaps will always remain, uncertain. Moreover, I distrust people who are too sure of themselves. I believe that a book which is open to uncertainty, what in deconstruction would be called the incalculable and the undecidable, is truer to the questioning side of human reason, and is a more trust-worthy guide because of this.

It also seems to me important to maintain plurality and neutrality in an introductory work. Eagleton's introduction to literary theory is extremely engaging; however, it is hard to imagine that it would ever induce anyone to take up the study of phenomenology or any of the other movements that Eagleton ridicules or dismisses. In this book I extend introductions on the principle that the ideas presented are ones the reader might actually someday wish to know better. Otherwise, why bother with introductions at all?

[handwritten annotation: how is the core best understood? appar. gone to status? the ... as to words.]

1

THEATRE, LIFE AND LANGUAGE

Semiotics, Phenomenology and Deconstruction

Much happens and many elements are at work on a theatrical stage: bodies, breathing, light, sound, movement, language and the material accidents and minutiae of existence. The range of such elements and their combinations are in many ways specific to theatre as an art form and cultural phenomenon. How is theatrical reality best understood? As life, embodiment, sensation, event, representation, meaning, a kind of writing? How does the nature of this reality limit the possibilities of theatre? What are the inescapable laws and fate of theatre? Different theoretical perspectives suggest different responses to these questions. In this chapter three such perspectives – semiotics, phenomenology, and deconstruction – are brought to bear upon the exploration of theatre as a specific and discrete reality.

[handwritten annotation: vrai]

1 SEMIOTICS

Semiotics is an important and trenchant place to begin a introduction to theory and theatre for a number of reasons. At least
two are especially noteworthy. First, the study of signs and
meaning, especially with its emphasis on the linguistic or
language-like character of all signification, has been as important as any movement in twentieth-century cultural theory,
informing developments in perhaps all subsequent areas of
theoretical endeavour. Second, because of its emphasis on
language over all else, and on signification over more visceral
activities, semiotics as much as any theoretical movement has
a problematic relationship to theatre and the understanding of
theatre. Do light, sound and movement always have meaning?
Isn't there a corporeality in theatre which is over and above the
presentation of meaning?

   Semiotics, or semiology, is the study of signs: words, images,
behaviour, human and animal arrangements of many kinds,
in which a meaning is relayed by a corresponding outward
manifestation. The falling leaves in autumn, for instance, are a
sign of the coming of winter. Almost all semiological work
in the twentieth century borrows basic tenets from Ferdinand
de Saussure's *Course in General Linguistics*. Saussure defines the
sign as having two parts: the signifier, which is the material
phenomenon we are able to perceive (the sound of a word, the
wave of a hand), and the signified, which is the concept
invoked by the signifier.[1] For Saussure, language is the most
characteristic semiotic system inasmuch as the relation
between signifier and signified is most arbitrary:[2] 'tree', 'arbre',
and 'Baum' have no necessary or essential connection to the
idea of a tree – unlike, perhaps (human duplicity enters in
here), the relation between a smile and the joy it expresses.
Saussure is most interested in internal linguistics, that is, he is
mainly concerned with language as a closed system more or

less unconnected to outside factors, to the world at large.[3] In this regard the signified is a concept and not a referent in the world – the idea of a tree rather than the tree itself. The real world does not impinge very much on Saussure's semiology. Neither, according to Saussure, do human beings think in a world as much as they do in language: 'our thought – apart from its expression in words – is only a shapeless and indistinct mass', and 'there are no pre-existing ideas, and nothing is distinct before the appearance of language'.

Because the linguistic signifier has no necessary connection to the signified concept or the real referent in the world, its significance is not grounded in anything very firm or positive. Words do not take their meanings from their relationship to ideas or things, but from their relationships with other words,[5] and these relationships are relationships of difference – 'tree' is tree because it isn't 'free' or 'thee' or 'tray'. This notion of difference, of a system without a transcendental unified term to give it coherence, without a sameness by which everything is measured, is central to much theory after Saussure and plays itself out in other areas: the psychoanalytic subject as different from itself; women as different from men or from each other; people of colour as different from and not reducible to standards of whiteness.

Saussure is interested in language not only as a closed semiotic system but also as an abstract system rather than as a system used by people in a changing world. He is more interested in *langue*, a particular language system, than in *parole*, the individual use of language in spoken expression,[6] or, by extension, particular acts of discursive expression in writing. Saussure is also more interested in the synchronic than in the diachronic aspects of language: in the abstract pattern of language as a system frozen in a moment of time rather than in history, change and event.[7]

The second founding figure of twentieth-century sign theory

is Charles Peirce, who called his field of study semiotics.[8] Peirce separates the sign (what Saussure calls the signifier) from the object, which is loosely what Saussure calls the signified, but a signified which can be in different situations a concept, a thing or even another signifier. He works out a classification of signs which sees them not as monolithic in the arbitrariness of their relationship to the object but as related to the object in different ways and to different degrees. A symbol – a word, for example – has an arbitrary relation to its object. An index, however – a finger pointing to indicate direction, for instance – has a closer relation to its object; an icon – a photograph of someone or an actor playing a part – has a strong resemblance to its object. Despite these gradations, Peirce insists, much as does Saussure, that a sign stands for something which is not present, thus reinforcing the absence and metaphysical hollowness that haunt all signification.

Peirce, unlike Saussure, is not so interested in sign systems apart from their deployment and insists that a sign is always a sign for somebody – in fact, that interpretation is part of the sign itself. In this way, semiotics is made situational, activated only by people in actual situations. Each act of interpretation begets another and leads to what Peirce calls 'unlimited semiosis', the endless play of meaning and regeneration of signs in time. This interest in interpretation and history makes Peirce's work quite different in emphasis from Saussure's.

The writings of the French theorist Roland Barthes are so wide-ranging that they could be discussed under a number of different rubrics; however, for the present discussion, Barthes is important for his applications of semiotic analysis to specific cultural activities and for his application of semiotic analysis to non-verbal as well as verbal signification. Barthes' early work is structuralist in its semiotic principles, seeking abstract models behind certain areas of cultural production ('Introduction to the Structural Analysis of Narratives'[9]) and imposing a linguistic semiological model on non-verbal activity – for instance, *The Fashion System*[10] is not concerned with clothing itself but with what is said about clothing; politically Barthes begins with a sense of 'myth', which is a semiological system whereby ideology is sweepingly imposed on a society.[11] Barthes' applications, or readings, of cultural activities, or texts, range from the minute analysis of literary texts (for example, Balzac's *Sarrasine* in *S/Z*[12]) to the analysis of forms of social discourse (the kinds of things lovers think and say in *A Lover's Discourse*[13]), to various popular icons (the face of Greta Garbo, the Eiffel Tower[14]), to systems of representation in painting and music.[15] These interests lead Barthes to question the relationship of language to non-linguistic activity. In general, he begins with a rather hegemonic view of language – for example, of *The Fashion System*, he says, 'fashion in its complex form, which alone interests us, exists only through discourse on fashion'.[16] 'Is Painting a Language?'[17] takes a slightly more open view of things. Late in his career, Barthes is more open still to the specific texture of non-verbal phenomena – the 'grain of the voice'.[18]

Over his career, Barthes moves from a reliance on structure as the imposition of an abstract model to an interest in structuration, which involves the specific and unique arrangements of cultural material in any particular instance. This involves a number of revisions: the idea of myth is replaced by the more heterogeneous and complex notion of codes; an interest in politics as imposition of 'the same old story' becomes an interest in the political – the myriad forms that relations of power take in everyday life;[19] work, as a fixed object to be read, becomes text, open to the endless play of interpretation;[20] the movement from work to text implies the death of the author as originary guarantor of stable meaning and the rise of the reader as activator of *jouissance*, an orgasmic joy in the unbridled dissemination of meaning;[21] Barthes moves from the abstract, scientific posture of structuralism to a rejection of science and metalanguage for the sake of an immersion in the language of texts themselves.[22]

Semiological studies of theatre have been undertaken by a number of theorists. A systematic and in many ways characteristic work of theatre semiotics is Keir Elam's *The Semiotics of Theatre and Drama*.[23] Elam displays the strong structuralist bent of much semiological analysis, attempting to provide a coherent system capable of accounting for all significant activity of theatre and drama: smiles, gestures, tones of voice, blocking, music, light, character development and so forth. Elam quotes the Eastern European semiotician Jiri Veltrusky: 'All that is on the stage is a sign.'[24] He presents elaborate charts to account for signification in the theatre and for the structures of signification in dramatic discourse: human affects, for instance, can be reduced to a complex system of gestures and tones. Theatre becomes eminently analysable and understandable, eminently readable. The sensual and experiential thickness of theatre (as will be discussed in the next section on phenomenology) becomes for semiotics a density of signs, denser and more complex than many sign systems, but a sign system nonetheless.

The French theorist Patrice Pavis has taken a somewhat different approach to theatre semiotics: a global systematization of theatrical signs is 'extremely problematic',[25] especially in the face of avant-garde theatre with a visceral distrust of meaning and signification.[26] A more manageable task for semiotic analysis is to study moments of theatrical signification 'on the fly', as it were, in all their localized specificity, without attempting to account for meaning in theatre as a totality.

In his short collection of essays, *Theatre Semiotics*, Marvin Carlson adds three concerns to the semiotic theory of theatre which he claims have been generally underdeveloped: the semiotic contributions of the audience to the meaning of a theatrical performance – in Peirce's terms, how the audience receives and interprets signs; the semiotics of the entire theatre experience – the 'appearance of the auditorium, the displays in the lobby, the information in the program, and countless other parts of the event as a whole'; and the iconic relationship of theatre to the life it represents.[27] Carlson's interests open semiotic analysis of the theatre onto relations with other theoretical approaches: his concern with the audience onto reception theory; his concern with the total theatrical experience onto materialist analysis; his interest in life on to phenomenology. Thus, for Carlson, these complications make 'performance potentially one of the richest and most rewarding areas in the arts for exploring the interplay of society and culture'.[28]

Brecht, Trauerspiel and Heiner Müller

Let us consider how some of these issues can be addressed in a particular theatrical instance. For Barthes, writing on theatre, the work of Bertolt Brecht is 'exemplary' for a semiological theatre: 'For what Brechtian dramaturgy postulates is that today at least, the responsibility of a dramatic art is not so much to express reality as to signify it.'[29]

Although Brecht's theory is not explicitly or directly influenced by semiotics, it is fairly easy to see what Barthes is getting at. Brecht's theatre is primarily concerned with meaning and understanding. Throughout his theoretical work, he stresses this aspect in a number of ways: his theatre is philosophical, scientific, intellectual, pedagogical.[30] The purpose of theatre is to put the audience in a better position to understand the world around them, a world which, for Brecht and Barthes, is social and changeable. The social world and its meanings, like Saussure's signs, are arbitrary but not un-motivated: they construct hierarchies of power for the benefit of the few and hide from the many their ability to change things (Barthes writes of the 'demystification'[31] of this misrepresentation in Brecht's theatre). A sign, therefore, is a social sign, what Brecht calls a *'gestus'*, and which Barthes defines as 'the external material expression of the social conflicts to which it bears witness'.[32] Imagine, for instance, being stopped for speeding by a member of the police. S/he approaches your car with an emotionless expression of authority and addresses you with a reserved, dominating correctness; you smile innocently, harmlessly and, sounding befuddled, address him/her deferentially as 'Officer': each of these artificial behaviours is a sign indicating the power relations and roles at play.

Barthes focuses on costume as one type of social sign: 'The costume is nothing more than the second term [the signifier] of a relation which must constantly link the work's meaning to its "externality"'; as such it must be constructed so as to aid in the reading of its social meaning. In this way theatre involves 'a politics of the sign'. Each theatrical *gestus* should aim for clarity of argument, in the case of costume for 'a precise vestimentary code', and the sensuous qualities of a costume, its grain and texture, are in the service of understanding, not sensuality.[33] Wealth, for instance, is not to be signified by piling on random luxury, but by presenting a careful and precise idea of vestimentary privilege.

The social *gestus* does not arise from an identity, a phenomenological closeness to being and doing; it is a role, one we agree to or are forced to adopt, and importance is placed in Brecht's theatre on alienation or internal distance from social meaning. Brecht takes his model of acting from social life, from the 'Street Scene' in which someone demonstrates an event – an accident, for instance, or an assault – not by becoming the person or action represented but by demonstrating it objectively from without:[34] think of a witness giving testimony at a trial. Theatrical action is explicitly representation rather than presence, and the actor has a double role on stage as both character and actor/demonstrator.[35] Theatre may be, as Pavis asserts, 'the privileged domain of the icon',[36] of signifiers with a close relationship to what they represent, but people and things on stage remain representations and are not identical to what is represented: the stage chair is not the chair represented, although it is a chair; the actor is not the character, although s/he is a human being.

For Brecht, as for Barthes, the generation of understanding and meaning is not an ascetic activity. Brecht writes of the 'pleasure of exploration', of a sensuous rationalism rich in humour, which is the most appropriate and viable pleasure in a scientific age. He writes, 'Every art contributes to the greatest art of all, the art of living.'[37] But living is a social activity, and its art is not about making present but about making a different and better world.

There is a tension in Barthes's reading of Brecht between a structuralist desire for system and a provisional and inductive openness. On the one hand, Barthes writes, Brecht 'offers not only a body of work but also a strong, coherent, stable system'; on the other, 'in Brecht's theater the Marxist elements always seem to be recreated. Basically, Brecht's greatness, and his solitude, is that he keeps inventing Marxism'.[38] Brecht is interested in inductive science, in which answers are discovered in particular situations rather than imposed systematically from the outset. In a later work Barthes argues that Brecht's theatre of discrete scenes means that there is 'no *final* meaning, nothing but projections, each of which possesses a sufficient demonstrative power'.[39] Nonetheless, for Barthes, Brecht's theatre controls and limits signs and meanings:

> The costume is a kind of writing and has the ambiguity of writing, which is an instrument in the service of a purpose which transcends it; but if the writing is either too rich, too beautiful or too ugly, it can no longer be read and fails in its function.[40]

Signs are instruments under human control; good theatre exercises this control in the service of understanding.

Semiotics does not always take, however, such an instrumentalist or functional view of the sign; nor does it necessarily believe that signification can be so controlled and limited.

A different view of theatrical signification can be seen in an early work of Brecht's friend Walter Benjamin (discussed more fully in Chapter 3), *The Origin of German Tragic Drama*.[41] Benjamin discusses the German baroque *Trauerspiel*, or mourning play, which he aligns with Shakespeare's *Hamlet* against classical tragedy. The *Trauerspiel* is allegorical, so that characters and objects are the signifiers for a range of emblematic meanings. The allegory, however, is not tightly controlled, but gives onto the 'free play of significances'; the allegory is ambiguous, lacking in clarity, and with a multiplicity of meaning.[42] The individual character is dispersed in multiple significance, and the stage object is incomplete and imperfect.[43] Not only is this a theatre of Peirce's 'unlimited semiosis', but also signs and allegory are not living expressions of human beings but an inhuman, mechanistic system with its own impetus. For this reason, the corpse is the 'pre-eminent emblematic property':

> the allegorization of the physis can only be carried through in all its vigour in respect of the corpse. And the characters of the Trauerspiele die, because it is only thus, as corpses, that they can enter into the homeland of the allegory.[44]

Humans are reduced to a function of signification, rather than, as in Brecht, signification reduced to an instrument of human purpose.

Barthes stresses the importance of Brecht 'for today', but even in the time of Barthes's reflections, in the 1950s, he sees that there are a number of ways of reading Brecht, from the right and the left, and also differently within each camp.[45] This understanding raises another question for theatre semiotics: the role of the audience in generating meaning. Peirce posits each act of signification as becoming in turn a sign in a new signifying context. In this light, some theorists of semiotics and theatre – for example, in the work of Carlson noted earlier – have come to stress the importance of audience reception for signification; Pavis, for example, notes 'the general trend of theatre semiotics, reorienting its objectives in the light of a theory of reception'[46] (more on reception and reader response in Chapter 2). How is it possible, in this situation, to control meaning down the line? How is it possible even at one time to control the multitude of meaning-making activities in a diverse theatrical audience? 'Unlimited semiosis' means not only the proliferation of meaning due to the nature of signs themselves, but also the proliferation of meaning among those who receive and generate signs. Brecht's theatre, as Barthes presents it, seems a very narrow, and perhaps impossible, example of signification in theatre, an example of control in the face of the infinite dispersal of significance.

Is it true, however, that everything on the stage is a sign, controlled or otherwise? Are there aspects of theatrical reality which are in excess of signification? In 1987 there was a production of Shakespeare's *Measure for Measure* at the Young Vic in London. For this production the stage was a square constructed of shiny black tiles in the centre of the audience. As people entered, there were stagehands to make sure that they did not walk across the stage to get to their seats, since the shiny stage caught every dusty shoe print. By the end of the night, however, the actors had transformed that polished pristine space into a smudged grey record of their every move- ment. Were these shoe prints theatrical signs? If so, what did they mean? One might see in them echoes of the inevitable corruption that haunts Vienna in the play. One might fault the director for allowing such wayward signifying noise to disrupt the clarity of the production. One might ignore them, as one ignores the idiosyncrasies of, for example, any particular stop sign, its dents and chipped paint. A perhaps inescapable drive of semiotics is to make of something a sign or otherwise exclude it from consideration. Aloysius van Kesteren, for example, from a highly scientific and rationalist semiotic perspective, calls for 'disinfecting' the discipline of 'non-analytical dirt'.[47] But what if non-analytical dirt is part of what is there on the stage or in the theatre? Shakespeare's original audience stood on earth rich in hazelnut shells and apple cores. In his essay on Gilles Deleuze, Michel Foucault (both discussed more fully in later parts of this book) approves of Deleuze's philosophical interest in 'the dirt under the fingernails of platonism'.[48] Not all or all that is interesting in theatre is allegory, understanding or sign. In reaction to the encroachment of semiotics, Jean-François Lyotard has called for a 'generalized desemiotics',[49] which would see theatre as energy and event rather than as signification. Like phenomenology, desemiotics is interested in the sensuous reality of theatre, but its drives are much more libidinous and visceral than phenomenology's contemplative relationship with the world.

If there is a politics of the sign, there is also a politics of desemiotics. For instance, the German playwright Heiner Müller, ambivalent disciple of Brecht, writes of the 'rebellion of the body against ideas', or 'the thrusting on stage of bodies and their conflict with ideas',[50] specifically the bodies of oppressed groups against the hegemonic and oppressive ideas of western male culture. Unlike Brecht, Müller does not see liberation in enlightenment rationalist values, but rather a long history of intellectualized injustice through the hegemony of the word. Irrationality, disorder and the senses promise more political liberation than does the strict control of meaning. But perhaps the fostering of western injustice and oppression is too great a guilt to lay at the feet of semiotics; conversely, a generalized desemiotics runs the risk of intellectual impoverishment: what richness is there in a theatre voided of meaning? Besides, the choice may be a phantom one. Ultimately, it is no easier to escape signs than it is to reduce all physical and theatrical reality to signification alone.

2 PHENOMENOLOGY

A theoretical approach extremely different from – if not diametrically opposed to – semiotics is that taken by phenomenology. Phenomenological concerns (developed in the philosophy of Edmund Husserl, Martin Heidegger and the early work of Jean-Paul Sartre, and in the literary criticism of Gaston Bachelard[51]) focus, in a way that sets them apart from much recent literary and critical theory, not so much on the social subject as on the individual consciousness, conceived in part as autonomous of social fabrication and capable of insight and reflection. Language is a concern of phenomenology inasmuch as language affects an individual's engagement with the world, but language is thought of more as an instrument for getting at truth than as a force for solipsism or ideology. There is less interest in the specifics of history as developed in materialist thought than in an at once more general and more personal idea of time. Phenomenology's primary concern is with the engagement in lived experience between the individual consciousness and the real which manifests itself not as a series of linguistic signs but as sensory and mental phenomena – the 'world' as encountered in perception and reflection rather than the 'earth' as things in themselves. In this way, the emphasis is on the presence or unconcealing of the world for consciousness rather than its absence through language, and therefore on the interplay with the real rather than its inevitable deferral. Phenomenology is concerned with truth, no matter how mediated, provisional and revisable. Especially in the work of Maurice Merleau-Ponty,[52] there is an emphasis on the manifestation of the world to the body as sensory apparatus which is absent in much language-based theory.

Although phenomenology posits the possibility of an authentic or fully human relation to the world, it is not naively rosy about such a relation coming about – the world is as often concealed as unconcealed, or unconcealed in counterproductive ways. Heidegger traces a history in which 'the way of technology' has progressed at the expense of a more poetic engagement with truth. Technology has turned the world, and humans themselves, into a 'standing reserve' in which everything and everyone is instrumental, a means to be used up or laid waste.[53] For Sartre humans bring nothingness to their consciousness of the world, and this sets them apart from things in themselves as 'not myself'. This gives radical freedom but also alienation and nausea.

For Heidegger, the work of art has a special relation to truth.[54] Unlike objects of utility or existence trapped in the day-to-day, works of art endure without being used up. They provide access, not to things in themselves, but to a privileged relation, of reflection and understanding, with the world, a relation usually concealed in other human activity.

Phenomenology has come under attack in much recent criticism as essentialist, and Heidegger, like the deconstructionist Paul de Man, has a very troubled reputation as a Nazi sympathizer. Terry Eagleton gives a particularly dismissive reading of phenomenology from a marxist perspective.[55] Nevertheless, phenomenology does treat lived experience in a compelling way, different from other theoretical perspectives and, taken with a healthy scepticism, it can be aligned with more political perspectives interested in embodiment and experience. Judith Butler, for instance, uses phenomenology in a feminist context.[56] The reading of Heidegger in the work of Gianni Vattimo provides a fusion of phenomenology with post-structuralist thought in which the perception of particular phenomena or beings goes hand in hand with the recognition of the absence of Being, the presence which no particular being can entail; phenomenology becomes the phenomenology of absence. In this reading, works of art are privileged instances of endurance in time, an endurance always marked by death, loss of origin, loss of self. Phenomena still reveal truth, but it is 'weak' truth, riddled with absence and adrift in time.[57]

Phenomenology has been applied to theatre in the work of Bert O. States.[58] He notes, for instance, the way certain beings on stage – clocks, chairs, children, animals – refuse to be strictly tied to representation and illusion (in *Monster in a Box*, Spalding Gray tells of a young boy actor vomiting during a performance of the final act of Thornton Wilder's *Our Town*[59]). Theatre works with vitality, corporeality – in short, life. Its primary accomplishment is not to represent the world but to be part of it, to effect a 'transaction between consciousness and the thickness of existence'.[60] Given day-to-day forces which rob us of our being present in our lives, the disclosure of theatre must be one of both presence and absence, but rather than deny the possibility of presence, as in much contemporary theory, States wishes to make it paramount.

Alice Rayner uses a phenomenological approach – although she also relies on Jacques Derrida and Jacques Lacan – to study action in theatre and drama. She attempts to get at the 'thickness' of action, its 'phenomenal complexity':[61] intention, agency, language and limit. She uses the conventional distinction between drama and theatre to pinpoint two aspects of action: giving shape and making visible. For Rayner, action itself (somewhat like Being for Vattimo) is a larger potential field or medium which theatre actualizes in particular circumstances; works of dramatic art, however, are also 'ways of seeing' which allow us to think through our relation to action and reality.[62]

Aside, most strikingly, from late nineteenth- and early twentieth-century experiments with marionettes in place of people (as in the theatre of Maurice Maeterlinck[63]), theatre has most often worked with the bodies of living actors on stage. Theatre is live theatre, or in the clarion-call of the 1960s experimental theatre of Julian Beck, 'The Living Theatre'. In a manner different from literary or pictorial arts, theatre has a special relationship to the presentation of lived experience. The sensory effects of light and sound in theatre are obviously open to phenomenological analysis. Furthermore, phenomenological concerns with embodiment can be seen in the ways that theatre sometimes works through sensory channels for extreme effects. In the 1970s, for instance, performance artist Gina Pane subjected herself on stage to painful self-laceration.[64] In the 1990s, the Toronto theatre company DNA, in a play called *Sick*, which dealt with the experience of AIDS, used the senses to impart to the audience a feeling analogous to illness: a tape loop repeated over and over at ear-splitting volume a short musical crescendo. After several minutes the audience member was inside the monotonous discomfort of the experience as the sick person is inside his or her pain. When the music suddenly stopped the inescapable difference between sickness and relief was made physically clear.

Stanislavski and Chekhov

What might be called phenomenological concerns figure prominently in the work of Constantin Stanislavski, whose autobiographical *My Life in Art* reveals a phenomenological bent in its very title.[65] 'My' speaks to the importance of individual experience and consciousness in the theatrical pursuit – the autobiographical form itself points to the importance of the individual life. 'Life', as in a phenomenological sense of fully engaged consciousness – what Stanislavski calls

'THE SUPERCONSCIOUS THROUGH THE CONSCIOUS'[66] – is of paramount importance to Stanislavski, but such life is most available 'in Art', in living theatre. When true theatre is taking place, 'the actor passes from the plane of actual reality into the plane of another life'; the actor creates life and 'the feeling of truth', incarnifies the human spirit, to the point of forgetting that he or she is on stage.[67] This process Stanislavski calls 'living over' a part.[68]

Stanislavski calls for a 'new beginning' to set against 'the outworn theatrical stencil' of wooden, lifeless, mechanical repetition, of lies and imitation.[69] In this way the stage is 'the ground of a battle between life and death'.[70] Unfortunately, although he writes of 'the Eternal in art', Stanislavski is saddled with an art form which has a distinctive relationship to time: 'a work of art born on the stage lives only for a moment, and no matter how beautiful it may be it cannot be commanded to stay with us.'[71] This is why a study of theatre such as this one of my own must always invoke references to performances long gone, which makes the study of theatre different from the study of literary or pictorial arts – as Stanislavksi says, 'the theatre cannot give the beginner such results as the library and the museum give to the writer and the artist'. The art of the actor is to recreate, which is not the same as repetition: repetition if mechanical is deadening; repetition of a moment of truth is impossible.

'Nature is unkind to man and rarely gives him what he needs in life,' Stanislavski writes.[72] He compares himself to Tantalus – 'I tried to reach something that forever escaped me'[73] – or to a gold-seeker who spends a lifetime to find a few precious grains. Theatre does not often match actual achievements to the loftiness of its goals.

Unlike the work of art phenomenology often invokes, theatre doesn't endure; but in this way it has a special elegiac relation to life, in which the past is gone and death awaits. As each performance slips away, so does each life and each person's knowledge and experience. Stanislavski writes, 'I cannot will to my heirs my labors, my quests, my losses, my joys and my disappointments', and

> nothing can fix and pass on to our descendants those inner paths of feeling, that conscious road to the gates of the unconscious, which, and which alone, are the true foundation of the art of the theatre. This is the sphere of living tradition.[74]

Stanislavski's most famous work was with the Moscow Art Theatre on the plays of Anton Chekhov. Almost equally famous is the sense of misunderstanding between Stanislavski's high-flown sensibility and Chekhov's irony. In Chekhov's plays we can see phenomenological concerns played out with more subtlety than in Stanislavski's often broad enthusiasms, this time on the level of theme and content.

Chekhov's plays have often been treated as naturalistic works immersed in the mundane details of Russian provincial life at the end of the nineteenth century. For Stanislavski, however, the plays addressed central concerns of art and theatre. Similarly, in 1959 the Polish director Jerzy Grotowski (discussed more fully later in this chapter) produced a very abstract *Uncle Vanya*, shorn of realistic detail, which concentrated on the distinction between alienation and convention on the one hand and spontaneity and life on the other, thus dwelling on the play's 'universal' meaning in 'a pure and aloof world of ideas'.[75] Moreover, Louis Malle's 1995 film of André Gregory's production of the play, *Vanya on 42nd Street*, although it featured a traditionally realistic approach to acting as identification with a specific character, was set in an empty theatre with no invocation of provincial Russia. Most striking was the way the actors were filmed as they eased into and out of their roles, so that the interplay between acting and non-acting was rendered problematic – at what precise moment and in what precise way do actors become or cease to be a character? It is this side of Chekhov's work, as theoretical reflection or enactment, which is the focus of the present discussion.

Chekhov's plays are filled with characters who feel they haven't lived, whose lives have been a kind of death. Masha begins *The Seagull* 'in mourning for my life'.[76] Sorin says, 'Twenty-eight years I've worked for the Department of Justice, but I haven't lived yet, haven't experienced anything – that's what it comes to.'[77] The two very different writers in the play, Treplev and Trigorin, are united in a similar sentiment. Treplev says, 'It's as if someone had banged a nail into my brain, damn it – and damn the selfishness that seems to suck my blood like a vampire', and Trigorin, 'I seem to see life and learning vanishing into the distance, while I lag more and more behind'.[78] In *Uncle Vanya*, Helen is 'bored to death', while Astrov says, 'As for my own private life, well, heaven knows there's absolutely nothing good about that'.[79] Vanya himself exclaims:

> Day and night my thoughts choke me, haunt me with the spectre of a life hopelessly wasted. I've never lived. My past life has been thrown away on stupid trivialities and the present is so futile, it appals me.[80]

Such feelings are expressed over and over again, in a special relation to time and repetition. *Uncle Vanya* begins with Astrov, worn out by ten years of labour 'from morning to night with never a moment's peace', and ends with Sonya forecasting 'a long succession of days and endless evenings'.[81] In between is Vanya, who has been 'cooped up in this place like a mole' for twenty-five years and wonders how he will fill the time he has left to live.[82] Bogged down in overwork or idleness, Chekhov's characters exist in a state of Heideggerian 'standing reserve', like the district forests – such a concern of Astrov – disappearing before the forces of utility and waste.

In *The Seagull*, Sorin imagines a short novel called *The Man who Wanted*, and lifelessness in Chekhov is tied to a longing for the fullness of existence: 'One wants to live, even at sixty', Sorin says.[83] Vanya longs 'to wake up some fine, clear morning feeling as if you'd started living again, as if the past was all forgotten, gone like a puff of smoke.'[84] People search for this new life in love affairs which always disappoint, in exciting locales like Moscow or Genoa, where 'You share its life, enter into its spirit and begin to think there really could be such a thing as a World Spirit',[85] in a nostalgia which forgets the discontents of the past. At the end of *Uncle Vanya*, Sonya seeks peace only in the afterlife, when 'We shall see all the evils of this life, all our own sufferings, vanish in the flood of mercy which will fill the whole world'.[86]

The most telling projection of life and happiness in Chekhov is into a distant human future. In *Uncle Vanya*, it is Astrov who thinks in these terms: 'Those who live a century or two after us and despise us for leading lives so stupid and tasteless, perhaps they'll find a way to be happy, but as for us – ', and projecting even more distantly, 'if man is happy a thousand years from now I'll have done a bit towards it myself'.[87] Visions of human happiness, of life fulfilled, remain compelling, but only through deferral; what endures in life is a radical postponement of living.

The Seagull begins with a theatre experiment at odds with the usual tenor of Chekhov's theatre: Treplev's drama of the 'World Spirit', which attempts to 'show life neither as it is nor as it ought to be, but as we see it in our dreams'.[88] Treplev rejects conventional theatre for 'a new kind of theatre'[89] in which souls will be united in a unified work of art. Stanislavski sees Treplev as a talented artist, 'with the soul of Chekhov and a true comprehension of art', set against the stencil of conventional realism represented by 'the worthless Trigorin'.[90] Chekhov's play, however, is much more ambivalent than this. To begin, Treplev's play is set – taking Chekhov's usual projections to extremes – 200,000 years in the future. But even then life has not triumphed: 'that will only come about after a long, long succession of millenia, when Moon, bright Sirius and Earth shall gradually have turned to dust. Until then there shall be horror upon horror.'[91] The distant future looks much like the present, only worse. Also, the play is framed by the failure of Treplev's work, its interruption in Act 1 and its empty stage, 'bare and ugly as a skeleton', at the end.[92] Finally, if Treplev's play is true theatre, what of Chekhov elsewhere, always mixing bathos with pathos, both ridiculous and compelling? *The Seagull* is neither Treplev nor Trigorin; it hollows out both dream and convention, promising fulfilment only as something that has not arrived and is not likely to. In this way, the phenomenology of Chekhov's theatre is like that of Vattimo, with the power of a weak truth and the presence only of deferral.

3 POST-STRUCTURALISM AND DECONSTRUCTION

Barthes's later work, with its movement away from system, abstract model and scientific principles, can be taken as post-structuralist, but nothing has marked the advent of post-structuralist thought as distinctly as Jacques Derrida's 'Structure, Sign and Play in the Discourse of the Human Sciences'.[93] Through a reading of the structuralist anthropology of Claude Lévi-Strauss, Derrida argues that structuralism is caught up in many of the philosophical assumptions it sets itself against, that this is necessarily so for any discourse in the western tradition, that there is no easy escape from this, that the unravelling of these assumptions must be slow and painstaking and opens up on a free play of signification which always already underlies any meaning and yet which all discourses, even those critical of philosophical certainty, tend in part to want to arrest. In a certain way, deconstruction takes such theories as semiotics, structuralism and phenomenology to their logical conclusions, even if the conclusions suggested differ from many of the aims these theories suggest to themselves.

Derrida's work is often called deconstruction, a process whereby the obfuscated and unacknowledged metaphysical assumptions (of truth, presence, identity, essence and so forth) and complicities of any particular text are unravelled from within and in the text's own terms. Deconstruction arises from an emphasis on the reading of particular texts, as opposed to general models, and from radical suspicion about the philosophic or scientific integrity possible in any piece of writing. However, on a more general theoretical level, Derrida is involved in what he calls 'grammatology' which is the study of the necessary effects of writing on any text.[94] Writing here means not only actual writing in all its forms but 'arche-writing', a process which underlies not only written but spoken language as well as thought, self and any activity taken to be text. And for Derrida, 'there is nothing outside the text'. This famous dictum has been taken in many ways, all of which are partly implied; for the present purposes, the following quotation, from a discussion of apartheid and South Africa, may serve as gloss:

> I found it necessary to recast the concept of text by generalizing it almost without limit, in any case without present or perceptible limit, without any limit that *is*. That's why there is nothing '*beyond* the text.' That's why South Africa and *apartheid* are, like you and me, part of this general text, which is not to say it can be read the way one reads a book.[95]

Everything – or at least everything humans deal with – is, for Derrida, text, that is, having the properties of arche-writing.

What are some of the characteristics of writing and textuality? For Saussure, difference is the relationship between signifiers, and Derrida takes difference to be at the heart of writing. He rewrites 'difference' as 'différance', meaning difference and deferral: nothing, no word, idea, text or subject, is what it was intended to be; nothing is identical with itself; the moment something is thought, said, written or intended, it becomes a trace of itself, no longer itself, no longer present; in this way, meaning, truth, identity, presence are always deferred and never arrive. Similarly, Derrida is involved in the undermining of any search for origins, for an earlier moment when thoughts, words, self and truth were identical and present to one another, when writing had access to the real and the truth. In this regard he also undertakes a critique of logocentrism, the belief that spoken language has more integrity than writing and that in speaking the separation of speaker and language is somehow avoided. The critique of the primacy of speech goes with a critique of presence, immediacy in all its forms, which entails not only an undermining of metaphysics but also of phenomenology's interest in the encounter between consciousness and reality.

Although Derrida says, 'history is not the last word, the final key, of reading', and that he is 'suspicious of the traditional concepts of history',[96] his notion of writing as iterable, as always displaced from its first situation into new and unforeseen circumstances, introduces the play of history into Derrida's analysis. Although he is not interested in the particulars of history – his usual unit of temporal analysis is the western epoch since the Greeks – his work entails a study of the conditions of historicity itself as endless iterability.[97] Related to iterability is Derrida's interests in translation and the inevitable differences that occur from one language or semiotic system or context to another.[98]

Finally, Derrida's suspicion of truth claims results in an extreme care and hesitance about coming to conclusions on intellectual, ethical and political questions. He asserts,

> And if I speak so often of the incalculable and the undecidable
> it's not out of a simple predilection for play nor in order to
> neutralize decision: on the contrary, I believe there is no
> responsibility, no ethico-political decision, that must not pass
> through the proofs of the incalculable or the undecidable.[99]

Related to undecidability is Derrida's belief that firm categorization – systems of genre, for instance[100] – are ultimately
untenable and undone by the uncontrollability and excess that
are part of any writing.

Aspects of deconstruction are enacted even more relentlessly
and single-mindedly in the work of Paul de Man. In a deconstructive reading of romantic poetry and thought, de Man
argues for a radical separation of language and nature: in any
approach to the world, there is the imposition of linguistic
and rhetorical structures which have nothing to do with
the natural objects under examination.[101] Similarly, de Man
radically separates intentionality and language: language
performs its rhetorical operations ultimately independent of
human agency.[102] While language is separate from nature
and human intention, its rhetorical structures unite all forms
of discourse: philosophy, as well as poetry, is caught in
misleading tropes which disallow the possibility of clear
thinking, while poetry, as well as philosophy, is capable of
deconstructing its own rhetorical blindness from within;[103] this
deconstruction slowly and never completely leads towards a
critical awareness of this blindness, which is the undoing, as
well as the most accomplished form, of the enlightenment
project and the investment in rational understanding.

One of many critiques of this way of thinking can be found
in the work of Jürgen Habermas, who is associated with the
Frankfurt School of 'Critical Theory', founded by Theodor
Adorno and Max Horkheimer. Habermas argues that the
enlightenment project must entail the work towards an 'ideal

speech situation' in which all distortions of ideology, institution, power and rhetoric have been understood and set aside so that rational exchange of truth can take place unhampered.[104] On the one hand, the ideal speech situation is a utopian idea which post-structuralist and deconstructive thought would take as an illusion and an impossibility; on the other hand, the assumption of the possibility of some rational exchange underlies even the relations of Derrida and de Man with their readers.

Deconstruction has been applied to theatre by Gerald Rabkin and Elinor Fuchs. Rabkin uses a variety of post-structuralist thinkers, most prominently Barthes and Derrida, to deconstruct authorial control and the stability of the written text in theatre, which give way to the 'dispersion, discontinuity and dissemination'[105] of open interpretation, especially in the hands of radical directors and troupes. Fuchs takes aim at the aura of theatrical presence that is often associated with live actors on stage and 'the theatrical enterprise of spontaneous speech with its logocentric claims to origination, authority, authenticity'.[106] In the place of speech and presence she posits a 'theatre of Absence' which 'disperses the center, displaces the Subject, destabilizes meaning'.[107] More recently, Stratos E. Constantinidis has attempted to systematize deconstruction as an analytical method derived from a 'skepticism which questions all kinds of interpretation',[108] especially around issues of authoritative consciousness, and has brought his somewhat idiosyncratic analysis to bear on a wide range of theatrical figures from Stanislavski to Sam Shepard.

Artaud, Grotowski and Blau

The most careful and exacting deconstructive work on theatre, however, has been done by Derrida himself. Derrida might well have chosen Chekhov as an exemplary object or model of theatre and deconstruction; like Chekhov, Derrida announces the coming of a future civilization, an epoch which will undo all the patterns of our own, but announces it only 'at a distance of a few centuries'.[109] In as much as deconstruction is in part an unravelling of phenomenological assumptions from within, Chekhov and Derrida partake of a common project. Be that as it may, Derrida has chosen to do his major study of the theatre in two very dense essays on the work of Antonin Artaud: 'La parole soufflée' and 'The Theater of Cruelty and the Closure of Representation'.[110]

Artaud's work combines a radical semiotics and a radical phenomenology. For Artaud, there is a 'rupture between things and words, between things and the ideas and signs that are their representation',[111] but this gap is to be overcome in a language of living signs:

> The objects, the props, even the scenery which will appear on the stage will have to be understood in an immediate sense, without transposition; they will have to be taken not for what they represent but for what they really are.[112]

In a theatre of unalienated signs, in which the arbitrariness and conventionality of social signification have given way to visceral and intellectual presence, we will be 'like victims burnt at the stake, signalling through the flames'.[113]

Artaud's language is laced with images of pain and cruelty. In part this arises from a phenomenological sense of having been separated from self or life: 'I am a man who has lost his life and who is seeking by every means to restore it to its place.'[114] Such restoration calls for drastic measures: 'The theater like the plague is a crisis which is resolved by death or cure.'[115] What is necessary in the theatre is 'the creation of a reality, the unprecedented eruption of a world'.[116] 'Theater must make itself the equal of life' – moreover it must take us 'where lives drink at their source'.[117] Such a theatre takes us beyond the standing

theatre
+ music

reserve of all social limitations and utility to 'an immediate gratuitousness provoking acts without use or profit'.[118]

One thrust of Derrida's reading of Artaud is to reveal the necessary paradoxes and contradictions in such thinking: signs by their very nature are representations and not the presence of what really is; there is no source or origin of life where human existence does not involve separation from itself. In 'La parole soufflée' Derrida argues that the living closeness of language, thought and self that Artaud envisions ultimately returns to the need for stasis and a fixed written text, which Artaud adamantly rejects elsewhere as the imposition of death and repetition; in 'The Theater of Cruelty and the Closure of Representation', Artaud's attempt to close and put an end to representation is seen to be inextricably bound up with the closure of representation in another sense: representation as the limit and unpassable horizon of possibility in the theatre.

This is not to say, however, that Derrida believes Artaud to have been a particularly careless thinker. On the contrary, according to Derrida, Artaud has gone further than anyone – perhaps even Nietzsche[119] – in unravelling western metaphysical thought from within, and he has done this by being more faithful to metaphysics than it is to itself.[120] Derrida's interest is in the margins and liminal areas of thinking where opposites share an entanglement, and he sees Artaud as working at the limits of western thought where there is an infinitely close complicity between metaphysics and difference, between error and truth, a complicity only made apparent by work at the limits. No one, for instance, has made as much of the limiting (or enabling) effects of language on thought, discussed by de Man, as has Artaud. Artaud writes:

> All writing is garbage.
> People who come out of nowhere to try and put into words any part of what goes on in their minds are pigs,

and

> I am truly LOCALIZED by my terms, I mean that I do not
> recognize them as valid in my thought. I am truly paralyzed by
> my terms, by a series of terminations. And however ELSE-
> WHERE my thought may be at these moments, I have no choice
> but to bring it out through these terms, however contradictory
> to itself, however parallel, however ambiguous they may be, or
> pay the penalty of no longer being able to think.[121]

Thus for Derrida, Artaud's writings are 'more a system of
critiques *shaking the entirety* of Occidental history than a treatise
on theatrical practice'.[122]

One reason that Artaud's writings are not so much a
treatise on theatrical practice is because of Artaud's close
connection with impossibility. For Derrida, the complicity
between metaphysics and the theatre of cruelty is a 'fatal
complicity',[123] inescapable and insurmountable, which 'obeys a
law': 'The transgression of metaphysics through the "thought"
which, Artaud tells us, has not yet begun, always risks return-
ing to metaphysics', even though Artaud's ultimate purpose
is the destruction of western civilization and thought and
the advent of a new epoch. Thus there is no way to create a
theatre beyond representation or with signs fully present to
themselves. Derrida demonstrates this by asking, 'Under what
conditions can a theater today legitimately invoke Artaud's
name?'[124] By a lengthy process of elimination, Derrida
concludes that no theatre can be what Artaud proposes: 'There
is no theater in the world today which fulfills Artaud's desire.
And there would be no exception to be made for the attempts
made by Artaud himself'.[125]

Certainly there is a discrepancy between Artaud's theoretical proposals and what he himself was able to achieve in
practice. Derrida's categorical relegation of theatre of cruelty to
impossibility, however, leaves us with the complex problem of

exemplarity in Artaud. Artaud often succumbs to the impossibility delineated by Derrida: 'Theater is the one thing in the world most impossible to save',[126] he writes, and asks, 'But who has drunk at the sources of life?'[127] And yet Artaud is always finding examples of the kind of theatre he is proposing: Strindberg's *The Dream Play*, Balinese theatre, Van Gogh's paintings, the Marx Brothers' *Animal Crackers* and *Monkey Business*, Jean-Louis Barrault's mime. It may be that the proliferation of examples is a compulsive response to Artaud's inability to make the theatre of cruelty a reality, but it might also be that, if we set our sights, as Artaud often does, below the absolute, it becomes possible to find intimations of the kind of theatre he is searching for. Towards the end of his life, Artaud sees in the radio broadcast of his own play *To Have Done with the Judgment of God* 'a small-scale model for what I want to do in the *Theater of Cruelty*'.[128] But it is on this small scale of theatrical practice that Derrida fails to address Artaud's project. Artaud sees himself labouring 'at the incandescent edges of the future',[129] neither mired in an impossible present nor fully arrived in a time yet to come. For all his torment, Artaud is much more optimistic – naively so – in his forecasting of the advent of the future than either Chekhov or Derrida: 'I shall be understood in ten years', he writes.[130]

The absoluteness of Derrida's concerns also undermine the carefulness of his reading of Artaud's politics. At its most sensitive and sophisticated, deconstruction brings an unrelenting interrogation to politics and decision-making. At its most cavalier, it jumps to the conclusion that political progress is impossible. In a note to 'La parole soufflée', most egregiously, Derrida draws a connection between Artaud's anal retentiveness – his mourning of the loss of self in loss of the faeces – and Marx's articulation of the alienation of the worker from his or her labour.[131] Derrida sees the connection as arising from a necessary metaphysics of alienation. But such a connection rides roughshod over important differences. For Marx, of course, workers are not alienated because they defecate, or even because their labour is externalized as work on the material world, but because of relations of production which rob and exploit them – externalization is not the same thing as alienation. Derrida leaves the significance of the connection he draws undeveloped, but this connection runs the risk of casting marxist politics into fatality and impossibility. Derrida's connection implies that there can be no political liberation as long as human beings have anuses; Artaud may possibly have believed that, but Marx, and many others, have believed otherwise.

A very different approach to Artaud from Derrida's can be found in the theorizing and theatre of the Polish director Jerzy Grotowski. Grotowski sees theatre as 'entering the age of Artaud',[132] but the task is to find concrete ways of carrying out aspects of what Artaud suggests – 'his idea of salvation through theatre',[133] for instance – while realizing that 'it is impossible to carry out his proposals'[134] and rejecting Artaud's sickness and imprecision. Grotowski works in 'confrontation' with Artaud, not as an obedient follower but as an adapter, taking up and remaking whatever is compelling and useful. What he adds to Artaud's project is a sense that acting and theatre are particularly disciplined and rigorous undertakings (in this thinking Grotowski is influenced by Stanislavski). In this way, Grotowski is able to take up a precise and particular task without the generalized sense of impossibility that Derrida brings to his reading of Artaud.

Grotowski's theatre takes place in the conjunction of opposites: spontaneity and precision, spirituality and physical rigour, theatre as both new testament and laboratory. Derrida's essays on Artaud make several references to the 'eve' of our own epoch or of an epoch to come. Deconstruction is interested in the 'eve' because it is a time when a new age has been announced but has not yet arrived and because it marks a marginal or liminal state when one thing is in the process of turning into its opposite – as Artaud's work is both the closing down and the inescapable enclosure of representation and metaphysics. Perhaps no 'eve' so plays with margins and opposites as does the Saturday before Easter, the eve of the Resurrection. Stanislavski, long before Grotowski, uses Easter as a recurring motif in his work for moments when theatre is reborn, but Resurrection's eve takes on a rich and deconstructive meaning in Grotowski's play *Akropolis*, which was filmed in 1968 for American television.

The Canadian theorist Northrop Frye, in his last book, discusses the importance of epitaphs for deconstruction. He writes:

> The most primitive form of visual poetry is the epitaph, which manifests Derrida's principle of *différance* very clearly. The epitaph typically says: stop and look at me; I'm dead and you're alive (difference), but you'll soon be dead too (deferral).[135]

But the relation of life and death on Resurrection's eve is more complicated than this. Christ is dead and death rules the world, but soon Christ will rise from the dead and live again. Is Good Saturday a time of life or death, or both? What if the Resurrection, like the new age for Derrida or Chekhov, is indefinitely postponed? It is in such a complex matrix that *Akropolis* is set. The play is based on an earlier work by Stanislaw Wyspianski, in which biblical characters depicted in a cathedral come to life on the night before the Resurrection. Grotowski transposes the action to Auschwitz and the characters to prisoners about to enter the ovens. The simple belief in eternal life or the progress of civilization is replaced by an intertwining of life and death: the acropolis, the height of western civilization, is equally the necropolis, the death camp, the cemetery of civilization. At the end of the play the actors, singing a Christmas carol at the top of their lungs, enter the oven in search of God and salvation.

In its staging, the play mixes the presence of bodies and life with the presence of death. The actors exhibit superlative physical power and presence, in extreme control of facial, gestural and vocal expression. There is a radical sense of their disciplined and focused presence as bodies acting. The biblical characters who come to life in Wyspianski's original, however, have been replaced by the lifeless fetish objects of the concentration camp: Christ is a headless rag doll; Rachel is a stove pipe; the hair of the dead is a strip of gauze or plastic – signifiers radically alienated from what they represent. Even the bodies of the living actors are tormented, twisted and shorn of their identities. As much as the play presents life, it presents life's absence. In making the spirit of the concentration camp live again, it recreates death and alienation, deferring resurrection on Resurrection's eve, and presenting rebirth as incineration and absence.

Deconstructive ideas are explicitly at work in the theatre and theory of Herbert Blau, who often refers to Derrida and deconstruction in his writing. What Blau draws from Derrida and elsewhere is a carefulness in working through complicity and illusion in theatre and theory, which are seen, in a manner reminiscent of de Man's interlacing of poetry and philosophy, as interrelated activities. Theatre is 'blooded abstraction' and 'metaphysics of the flesh', while theory combines a performative impulse with an antitheatrical ideational prejudice.[136] Thus, *Elsinore*, Blau's adaptation of Hamlet, is labelled an 'analytic scenario', while *Crooked Eclipses*, his adaptation of Shakespeare's sonnets, is a 'theatrical essay'.[137]

Blau's theatrical and theoretical work involves the 'sounding' of the subtle distinctions and the vertigo of seeming and truth in any attempt to clarify and understand the human and theatrical condition: 'the unremitting meticulousness of the thinking through of illusion'.[138] This involves Blau in many of the conundrums mapped out by deconstruction. Is theatre, for instance, a place of presence or what Blau calls 'ghosting'? The idea of immediate and unmediated presence is an illusion, and the body is always ghosted with words – indeed performance seems written even when there is no text.[139] However, it would be equally illusory to think of the actor as entirely absent. The actor, like every human being, is a thinking body performing blooded thought. As an actor says in *Elsinore*, 'I saw my body ... and how I couldn't get out of it'.[140] In this inescapable struggle between blood and thought, theatre enacts the problem of western metaphysics.[141]

Intellectually, Blau combines relentless suspicion and unremitting commitment, both of which he sees in Shakespeare. *Hamlet*, for instance, presents thought so dense it 'feels, structurally, like brain damage'.[142] Here we are given a sense of deconstruction's hopelessness vis-à-vis the human capacity to see clearly past illusion to the heart of things. In this way, Blau's thought and theatre resemble the thought of de Man. On the other hand, a key moment in *Crooked Eclipses* involves the actor Ellen, 'kneeling, speaking simply to somebody in the audience', speaking the sonnet 'Let me not to the marriage of true minds / Admit impediments'.[143] Here, no matter how circumscribed by illusion, is the enactment of a moment of ideal communication like that envisioned by Habermas.

Blau's politics are equally conflicted. He sees 'a virtually irremediable split between art and politics' and sees in Heiner Müller's collaboration with Robert Wilson on *Hamletmachine* the solipsistic babble of a defeated politics.[144] And yet Blau remains 'messianic about the theater, ... in it to create the possibility of a valid public life, to save the world in fact'; if reality makes that seem impossible, then Blau will work for change despite the forces of reality.[145]

In this chapter, through semiotics, phenomenology and deconstruction, we have asked if there is a fundamental reality to theatre, what Stanislavski calls the laws of nature that lie behind theatre, or Derrida calls the necessity that underlies all textuality. Is there an essence to theatre? Is it as sign, lived experience or text? Does theatre have a multiple reality, so that it is sign, lived experience, word and body, absence and presence, and much more, all at once? How can we articulate the connections and inevitable contradictions between different ways of thinking about the nature of theatre?

Moreover, if we were to come to some understanding or conclusion about this reality, where does this leave the theatre artist? Is the reality of theatre such as to arrest all work in a necessary fate, to defeat the possibility of many, if not all, theatrical projects? Or is there space, in the interstices of over-lapping realities, to make theatre happen, no matter how incompletely and momentarily? What do the great laws and necessities of theatre mean for the specific performances of theatre artists in the world? Does theatrical reality create a limiting necessity or a space of structured possibility?

These are some of the questions we are left with in the face of theories which try to explain the nature of theatre. Such theories may clarify the theatrical predicament and hone our questioning, but they will not make such questions go away.

Finally, this chapter for the most part has dealt with theatre as a closed system set apart from other concerns and activities. As I said in the introduction, this does not imply that semiotics, phenomenology and deconstruction having nothing to say about theatre in relation to these other concerns and activities – quite the contrary. Nor do I wish to imply that theatre ever can be completely set apart from the rest of life and society. There is a procedure in phenomenology called 'bracketing', whereby certain concerns are bracketed or set aside so that consideration can focus on a more limited set of questions. In this chapter I have, in effect, bracketed off concerns of subjectivity and the social sphere discussed more fully in the next two chapters;

in doing so, however, I must stress that they are set aside only temporarily and artificially, and any understanding that strives for fullness must always be prepared for their inevitable return. A full discussion of Chekhov, for instance (one of many possible examples), would need to examine the historical and social, as well as the phenomenological, grounds of disappoint-ment, and a full discussion of Artaud would need to discuss his anti-Americanism and anti-imperialism and in consequence his affinity with post-colonial thought.

2

SUBJECTIVITY AND THEATRE

Psychoanalytic, Gender and Reader-Response Theory

JOAN AS DIONYSUS Good evening. I see you found your seats. My name is Joan MacIntosh, daughter of Walter MacIntosh and June Wyatt. I was born twenty-three years ago in a hospital in Newark, New Jersey. I have come here tonight for three very important reasons. The first and most important of these reasons is to announce my divinity. I am a god. The second of these reasons is to establish my rites and rituals. As you can see, they are already in progress. And the third is to be born, if you'll excuse me.[1]

In Chapter 1, I discussed the living body of the human being as it exists in theatrical activity. But whose body are we talking about? There are any number of human beings involved in specific capacities in making theatre. In drama, there are the author, the reader and, in a fictional sense, the characters; in theatre, there are the director, the actors, the technicians and the audience. We can add the drama or theatre critic to this mix. If we think collectively or relationally of all those involved, then we need to consider each human being not only in his or her particular role but as part of a complex whole. And we can posit this whole in larger or smaller ways: from a whole society or cultural formation to those in attendance at one theatre on one particular occasion.

Much recent theory has focused on two specific terms to understand who human beings are and what they do. The first term is 'subject', and it implies (most specifically in the work of the marxist theorist Louis Althusser) two contradictory qualities. First we are subjected in the sense of moulded, fashioned, made to someone or something else's orders, whether that someone or something else is the father or patriarch in psychoanalysis and feminism or capital in marxism. To be a subject, therefore, is to be something other than free or autonomous, something other than self-created or independent of others. But subject also implies, in grammar or liberal political theory, a doer, capable of independent action and self-direction. To some degree, the first sense of subject gives the lie to the second, or at least indicates its profound limitations. But does our subjectedness completely limit our subjective freedom? The second important term is 'agent', that which has power to act or effect something, and in many ways the idea of the agent is tied up with the idea of the subject in the second sense. The idea of agency, however, has tried to avoid some of the naivety in the idea of the autonomous individual. The agent can only act in its position as subjected and therefore has only very limited power and autonomy. Also, given our subjection to others, it may be that our fullest agency is as part of a group, which gives us necessary direction and support, rather than on our own.[2]

In this chapter I have chosen to focus on three theoretical movements in order to explore questions of subjectivity and agency as they apply to those involved in making theatre. The first theoretical movement is psychoanalytic theory, which attempts to understand how human beings become the way they are and why they act in the ways they do. The second movement is gender theory, which includes feminist theory as well as gay and lesbian theory and what has most recently come to be called queer theory. Like much psychoanalytic theory, gender theory stresses the importance of sexuality in human identity, but it often takes a more contestatory and liberatory stance towards the possibility of making ourselves over in new and more satisfying ways. Finally, I look at reception or reader-response theory. In running reception and reader-response theory together, I am doing a disservice to sophisticated and somewhat distinct theoretical approaches; I do this because there is something to be gained for theatre studies in thinking of these two schools as part of one large concern: the mapping of those involved in making cultural significance. In the reading of a book, it might be said, there is an interchange between only two subjects: author and reader. A more sophisticated and historicized reception theory would note that book publishers, teachers, critics and many others haunt this interchange. In the theatre, however, it is much more apparent that what happens is the responsibility of many human forces: a director who cuts a scene; an actor who flubs a line or gives an idiosyncratic reading; an audience that laughs or doesn't laugh; a critic whose bad review effectively shuts down a production and fixes its failure in the public record.

Once again, a few caveats are in order before we begin. As in Chapter 1, the three theoretical approaches chosen do not exhaust the exploration of the issues at hand. Phenomenology, for instance, or materialist theory have much to say about the human being. Nor should it be assumed that feminism, for instance, only speaks to the concerns of subjectivity raised in this chapter. Also, my discussion at the beginning of the section on reception theory points out the complex intersections with other theories which make any particular theory possible. Such intersections must at times retreat into the background, but they should not be forgotten.

1 PSYCHOANALYTIC THEORY

Psychoanalytic theory is concerned with the way that the psyches of human beings are formulated. The first and most important name in psychoanalytic theory is Sigmund Freud.[3] Freud's work is far-ranging and detailed, but we can extract the following important basic principles: the human psyche is constructed; the human psyche is segmented; the human psyche is gendered. The constructedness of the human psyche is seen in the stages of development (oral, anal, genital; pre-oedipal, oedipal) that it undergoes, as well as in the range of normal and 'aberrant' outcomes that are possible for psychic development (heterosexual, homosexual, bisexual; neurotic, psychotic, etc.); human beings are not so much born as made. The segmentation of the subject is seen in various topologies Freud proposes over the course of his career, such as the division of the psyche into superego, ego and id, or the separation of the conscious and the unconscious: the human psyche is not one entity fully present to itself as consciousness but rather a divided and largely unknowable complex. For Freud, all psychic development is gendered, and males (are allowed to) develop differently from females; the presence or absence of the penis allows for the development of very different identities and ways of being in the world. These differences are controlled by the 'oedipal' patterns whereby we are slotted into various sexual and familial roles as father, mother, son and daughter.

Much of the nature of the psyche as constructed, segmented

and gendered is not immediately apparent and can only be apprehended – like the workings of the unconscious – through careful analysis of dreams and certain linguistic phenomena; much of Freud's work maps ways of uncovering the psyche's hidden truths.

In *Beyond the Pleasure Principle*, Freud tells a story concerning his grandson, who compulsively acts out the coming and going of his mother by concealing and revealing a wooden top, while announcing '*fort*' [gone] or '*da*' [there]; in this way the child comes to grips with the absence and presence of important objects in the outside world, with gratification and deprivation.[4] In the study of 'object relations', the relations between the psyche and the others (people and things) that are important to it, psychoanalytic theory suggests a particular understanding of human relations with the outside world.

Freudian psychoanalytic theory is further developed in the writings of Jacques Lacan. Following semiotic and linguistic theory (discussed in Chapter 1), Lacan stresses the importance of language for the human psyche.[5] Not only is the unconscious – in Lacan's famous formulation – structured as a language[6] (Lacan rewrites Freud's condensation and displacement, the mechanisms whereby associations work in the unconscious, as metaphor and metonymy, concepts borrowed from the linguistic theory of Roman Jakobson), but the subject becomes a chain of signifiers – the human psyche becomes for all intents and purposes a linguistic entity.

The linguistic subject engages with itself and the world in one of two registers: the imaginary or the symbolic. The imaginary is an inflexible and delusory state associated with infancy and later various arrested or psychotic conditions; the symbolic entails an engagement and dialogue open to change and development and is associated with effective socialization. What escapes these registers is the real, which exists independently of language and is therefore inaccessible to language and

the linguistic subject (this bears much similarity to the re
between reality and language outlined by Paul de Man).
Freud, the subject also harbours an unconscious which remains
inaccessible to itself except indirectly through its effects. The
unconscious is the discourse of the 'Other', that part of a subject
which is 'not I' and which renders every subject alien from
itself. (The idea of the 'Other' is a very resonant idea in Lacan,
and is also extremely important, *mutatis mutandis*, for feminism,
post-colonialism and gay and lesbian studies, which seek to
identify with that which is other than white, male and heterosexual, a nexus taken as politically and ideologically dominant
in the world.) Because we have no direct access to the real or
to our own unconscious, the subject is bound to a certain
'*méconnaissance*', a mistaking or misknowing. Truth, as for
Derrida and de Man, is humanly impossible.

Lacan also changes the penis as Freud understands it into
a linguistic entity: the phallus, which is not an actual penis,
but a linguistic idea, a transcendental signifier which holds
in place the possible and acceptable exchanges between
linguistic subjects. As for Freud, males have a different relation
to subjectivity than women do, since there is a metaphorical
resemblance between the penis and the phallus which causes
males to be able to misrecognize themselves as aligned with the
phallus as site of power and authority – the 'law of the father'.
The change from penis to phallus makes a number of differences for the theory of gender in Lacan. Most importantly,
differences of gender are no longer biological but linguistic and
symbolic. Whether the move from biology to language makes
any real difference is a contentious point, however, as can be
seen in the two introductions to *Feminine Sexuality*, a collection
of essays by Lacan and his '*école freudienne*'. In her introduction,
Juliet Mitchell sees the phallus as constituting a kind of fate:
there is no subjectivity outside of the relation to the phallus and
therefore outside of masculinity and femininity; for Mitchell

there is no subjectivity or even civilization without the phallus and the law of the father. On the other hand, Jacqueline Rose in her introduction argues that the distinction between penis and phallus renders male identification with the phallus illusory, and this opens up a space of play and liberty, especially associated with the feminine as free of any such deluded identification, and the possibility of subjectivity and exchange beyond the phallus and the law of the father.[7]

Julia Kristeva is an important figure in feminist theory, but her *Revolution in Poetic Language* can also be taken as an important and systematic contribution to psychoanalytic thought.[8] According to Kristeva, human beings begin in the state she calls 'semiotic'. By this she means something quite different from what Saussure means. The semiotic is a pre-linguistic order associated with the mother's body, with a space of heterogeneous drives and desires, with the feminine. In coming to language, the subject enters the 'symbolic' order, associated not only with language but also with reason, law, the father and the masculine. In entering the symbolic order, the human becomes the 'thetic' subject, and turns away from the body, the mother and the rhythms of desire; but this loss is accompanied by access to the power of language, reason, society and the law. The story does not stop here, however: the semiotic, which never goes away, returns to disrupt the imaginary unity and coherence of the thetic subject. Through irruptions of desire, rhythms, language not bound by linearity, syntax and reason, the semiotic negates and renews the thetic subject, which becomes a subject in process or perpetually on trial. The subject in process is a subject always becoming in the never-ending and heterogeneous dialectic of semiotic and symbolic forces. In her studies of literature, Kristeva looks for 'revolution in poetic language', the irruption of semiotic desire and non-syntactic rhythms in symbolic language.

Kristeva is also known for developing the idea of 'inter-textuality': all writing takes place in the web of texts that come before and after it. Any text is always replete with, even written by, others' texts, just as any subject is constituted in language not its own.

The work of Gilles Deleuze and Félix Guattari, like that of Kristeva, covers a wide range of concerns and is classifiable in a number of ways. The two volumes of *Capitalism and Schizo-phrenia*, *Anti-Oedipus* and *A Thousand Plateaus*,[9] are concerned with the rethinking and liberation of the human entity. Deleuze and Guattari see humans as presently oppressed and stultified in the relations between oedipal psychic structures, capitalism and the monolithic state. Their work points towards a future in which de-oedipalized, deterritorialized and deregulated humans are free to become something other, free to travel a thousand plateaux. This other is formulated in different ways: becoming-woman, becoming-animal, becoming-machine. These becomings entail first of all a different relation to the body: Deleuze and Guattari posit a human entity without a face – to the degree that our notion of face locks us in a certain sense of individuality; they also take up Artaud's notion of a 'body without organs', a body not subjected to organization and hierarchy. New human entities also take up different relations to language and thought – animals, for instance, are driven by drives and desires rather than laws and ideas.

Deleuze and Guattari also promote a different possible relation to the real. They call for an understanding based on mapping, 'entirely oriented toward an experimentation with the real', rather than tracing, which reduces multiplicities to known patterns.[10] In this way their thought is different from that of Lacan. Also, unlike Derrida or de Man, Deleuze and Guattari believe in the possibility of the alignment of an ontology of difference with a liberatory politics: a world founded on the eternal recurrence of difference leads, if not directly then insistently nonetheless, to a politics of unfettered becoming. Politically, they are concerned with the tactical distribution of ontological difference.

In literature (and theatre), Deleuze and Guattari are interested in the 'minor', which undoes oedipal and capitalist patterns from within a 'major' tradition by multiplying and unravelling patterns of oppression until they lose any sense of unity or centre.[11] This process of deterritorialization, however, must be done with a slow and meticulous care rather than with precipitous and destructive haste.

Very important psychoanalytic work on drama has been done by both Freud and Lacan. *Oedipus Rex*, *Hamlet* and the two parts of *Henry IV* serve important, even primary, explanatory and illustrative functions in Freud's development of the oedipus complex and of dream logic.[12] Lacan has developed extensive readings of *Antigone* and *Hamlet*.[13] These analyses serve as the *loci classici* of the psychoanalytic interpretation of theatre.

Psychoanalysis has dealt with art and literature mainly in three ways. The first is to use the art to psychoanalyse the artist, as if the art were a symptomatic document like a dream or a slip of the tongue. Freud uses this approach to study a work by Leonardo da Vinci,[14] and analyses of such an artist as Franz Kafka are commonplace. The second approach psychoanalyses the characters in order to draw out compelling examples of psychic mechanisms and patterns at work – Oedipus and Hamlet become primary examples of oedipalization. Finally, a text can be read not for its insights into the particular psyche of author or character, but as demonstrating the patterns of, say, the linguistic psyche in general. Lacan's reading of Edgar Allen Poe's 'The Purloined Letter'[15] falls into this category; similarly James Joyce's *Finnegans Wake* can be read as revealing the structures of 'everybody's' dream life.

As drama text, theatre is open to each of these approaches.

dream text
performers
interval

Any playwright or dramatic character is susceptible to psycho-analytic analysis, and in the realm of character, drama has yielded particularly rich material for psychoanalysis. Shakes-peare's *A Midsummer Night's Dream* or August Strinberg's *Dream Play* can be read as works which explore the mechanisms of the psyche itself. A fourth possible approach is to bring psychoanalysis to bear on a cultural formation or institution; for example, one could study the psychoanalytic effects of classical Greek theatre or modern American theatre.[16] This fourth approach stresses the social and performative aspects of a cultural practice like theatre, and this performative aspect is often especially underdeveloped in predominantly literary studies.

Classical psychoanalysis deals with verbal symptoms, but it is only actualized in the analytic situation, with the enactment of the analysand in the presence of the analyst, with the emo-tional investments of transference and countertransference, and the repetition of sessions at regular intervals. Analysis so described is obviously a performative practice as well and has much in common with theatre. Literary psychoanalysis, under the influence of Lacan – notorious for ever shortening the psychoanalytic session – has made relatively little of the performative relations between psychoanalysis and theatre. The recent psychotherapeutic movement of 'dramatherapy', however, has made theatre central to its understanding of the human psyche. Here the concept of 'role', which 'applies to the full range of human experiences through body and sensorium, mind and emotion, intuition and spirit',

> provides coherence to the personality, and . . . in many ways
> supersedes the primacy of the concept of self. And by extension,
> existence is not only played out as in a drama, but is dramatic in
> its own right.[17]

In many ways, dramatherapy harkens back to the classical and

Renaissance idea of *theatrum mundi*, the theatre of the world, in which the world is thought of as a stage and, in Shakespeare's words, 'all the men and women merely players'. This is a very complex idea which draws often contradictory and unsettling connections between theatre and human identity. Is there a real self behind the role? Is acting a form of deception? Or is role-playing our natural and inescapable means of being in the world and expressing ourselves?

Spalding Gray

A psychoanalytic study would have to work on a number of the levels outlined above in order to understand a phenomenon like Spalding Gray's theatrical monologues. Gray has performed a number of autobiographical monologues in which he sits at a table with notes and a glass of water and recounts incidents from his life, often linked to and by his forays into the film world (as in *Swimming to Cambodia*, which deals with Gray's experiences while at work on Roland Joffe's film *The Killing Fields*). Although partly dealing with Hollywood, Gray's *Monster in a Box* is a work in which he discusses the problems – mainly psychological – he had completing his novel, *Impossible Vacation*. *Impossible Vacation* is dedicated to Gray's mother, 'the Creator and Destroyer', and the novel focuses on the thinly veiled fictional protagonist's inability to leave his mother and take a vacation while she is alive and even more so after her suicide.[18] *Monster In a Box* makes explicit the identification of Gray with his protagonist and deals with Gray's inability to write this novel about events before and after his mother's death.[19]

Both *Impossible Vacation* and *Monster in a Box* deal with obviously psychoanalytic material: love for and the attempt to escape from the mother, sexuality, guilt, transference and cathexis, the inability to escape the traumas of the past, and the working through of psychological difficulties. If anything, these matters are eminently transparent: Gray wears his psychoses on his sleeve. The preface to *Monster in a Box* tells how, after a performance of the play, Gray was asked to be the national spokesman for the National Foundation for Mental Health, because he was 'so articulate about [his] mental illness'.

A seemingly simple performance such as *Monster in a Box* leaves us with many unanswered or unanswerable questions. For instance, who is Spalding Gray? The playwright is Spalding Gray, the character is Spalding Gray, the actor is Spalding Gray. Are these three one and the same? Is the actor who speaks the lines at one with the voice of the author? Much current theory would tell us that the author is, in effect, dead before the actor starts to speak. When the actor speaks, is he the Spalding Gray he claims to be? If we answer yes, are we saying that there is nothing fictional about the character Spalding Gray? Is playing oneself on stage the same as playing oneself offstage? Isn't it in the nature of dramatic characters to be unreal? Gray (which Gray, though?) claims that he invents nothing: 'I don't know how to make anything up. . . . I don't know how to tell the lie that tells the truth – I can only tell what happened to me.'[20] Freudian analysis is built on suspicion: we always distort what we say about ourselves. Therefore, both theatre and psychoanalysis tell us that Spalding Gray cannot simply be who he says he is. And yet, can we say that Spalding Gray the character simply is not Spalding Gray the actor or playwright? Isn't our reception of Gray's work premised on a belief that all the Spalding Grays are in some sense the same? What would happen if an actor other than Spalding Gray were to play Spalding Gray? Would *Monster in a Box* then be the same kind of performance?

Gray relates taking on the role of the stage manager in Thornton Wilder's *Our Town*: 'I could speak from my heart at last, provided I could memorize the lines – and I could use my New England accent.'[21] Is playing the stage manager completely different from playing oneself? In some way Gray can identify with a role other than Spalding Gray, so that the role of the stage manager isn't simply other than Spalding Gray. The role an actor takes on cannot be simply other any more than one can simply be oneself. Acting has a topology just as the psyche does: we can divide Spalding Gray into id, ego and superego or, in another context, we can divide Spalding Gray into playwright, character and actor. These are not the same topologies; theatre is not a straightforward homology of the psychoanalytic self. Both theatre and psychoanalysis, however, make clear that human beings are neither monolithic nor transparent.

At one point in his story, Gray finds himself undergoing traditional Freudian analysis:

> Now we're working very fast and very hard, and I'm telling him the story of my book. Certainly I know what the cure in psychoanalysis is supposed to be, so I'm looking both ways. I don't want it to take me by surprise because I'm not really sure I want the cure. I know the cure is supposed to be the transformation of hysterical misery into common unhappiness. And God knows I have a lot of hysterical misery, but I'm not sure I want to let it go.[22]

If analysis is the talking cure which through performance takes one past or through one's pyschic arrest, what purpose do performance and repetition in theatre serve? *Impossible Vacation* features an epigraph from William Kennedy's *Ironweed*: 'You will not know . . . what these acts are until you have performed them all. . . . Then, when these final acts are complete, you will stop trying to die because of me.' The novel presents a series of acts through which the protagonist cures himself of his inability to get past his attachment to his mother. In *Monster in a Box*, the writing of the novel serves a similar therapeutic function. But what of the performance of *Monster in a Box* itself? Gray creates his theatre pieces by letting them evolve through a series of outlined but unscripted performances. When the process is complete, the text is written down and the performances end. Is this too a therapeutic process? What cure does it entail? Didn't the writing of the novel effect the necessary psychic healing? If so, what does the play do? And what of Gray's desire to hold onto his hysterical misery? Does performance repeat and preserve that misery as much or more than it dissipates it? Perhaps *Monster in a Box* serves no therapeutic role at all, and the performance process is about getting the art right, not the person. In this regard, there is something strangely distant and dispassionate about Gray's performance, as if the stories he tells don't matter to him anymore – almost as if they had happened to another person.

Dionysus in 69

Herbert Blau speaks of 'our oedipal drama',[23] by which he means that theatre, like ourselves, is caught in the structures of identity, family, desire, misrecognition, repression and so forth delineated by Freud and psychoanalytic theory. Gilles Deleuze, in 'One Less Manifesto', a discussion of the theatre of the Italian playwright, director and actor Carmelo Bene, outlines some of the institutions and connections whereby theatre is tied to oedipalized society: language in the theatre is the oedipalized language of the master (king, father or patriarch); the author is a figure of authority, overseeing the proceedings as a kind of superego; the actor, gendered and fixed in a societal role, takes up the role of a character similarly conceived of as a fixed psychological individual; within the play lead characters duplicate societal hierarchy in their mastery over lesser characters.[24] Deleuze is interested in Bene because Bene is interested in breaking down these complicities, in creating an anti-oedipal theatre. Bene attempts this through disruptions of standard theatrical elements: language becomes noise, character becomes chaos, scenography is free of the master's control.

While Blau and Deleuze would agree that theatre is oedipal, they would disagree profoundly on the possibility of escaping this condition and on the virtue in doing so. For Blau, to think you can escape oedipal structures of desire and identity is an illusion, and cavalier attempts to do so can be both intellectually and societally dangerous.

Some of these oedipal and anti-oedipal tensions can be seen in the Performance Group's *Dionysus in 69*, a quotation from which serves as epigraph to this chapter. *Dionysus in 69* is a retelling of Euripides' *The Bacchae*, in which Pentheus is torn to pieces by his mother, Agave, induced to frenzy by Dionysus, the god of excess and disorder. The play deals with forces which break oedipal bonds of selfhood, family, sanity, even the unity of the human body. *Dionysus in 69* was produced in 1969, part of a countercultural movement interested in the waylaying of oedipal repression through individual and group liberation, nudity, openness and political and sexual experimentation. Did it succeed?

The quotation at the head of this chapter shows some of the tensions involved: the actress Joan MacIntosh is first positioned oedipally as daughter of Walter MacIntosh and June Wyatt: she is an individual much like the rest of us. But she is also to be a god, and not just any god, but Dionysus, who induces ecstatic frenzy which takes people out of themselves. And yet, will such role playing really allow Joan MacIntosh to escape herself in any way at all? A similar quandary confronts the liberationist sexual politics of the play, which climaxes with an orgy staged by the actors among the audience: would-be Lotharios in the audience took this as an occasion to touch the actresses in ways the actresses were not comfortable with. Remember also that at the end of *The Bacchae*, Pentheus's mother comes to her senses and realizes the horror of what she has done.

A perspective in many ways akin to Blau's can be found in the work of the East European theorist Slavoj Žižek. Žižek has written a number of books elucidating the theories of Lacan with reference to examples from popular culture, most prominently from the films of Alfred Hitchcock. There are relatively few references to theatre in Žižek's work, and most of those are to the standard psychoanalytic pantheon (Sophocles' Oedipus plays, *Antigone*, and Shakespeare's *Hamlet*) or to Bertolt Brecht. Also, the title of his *Looking Awry* is taken from a scene in Shakespeare's *Richard II*.[25] Žižek's readings are rarely detailed and, strangely for a Lacanian, take more interest in character, theme and ideas than they do in language. It would be possible, nonetheless, to substitute theatrical examples for the cinematic citations that pepper his work. More generally, Žižek's work might inform a study of our need to make meaning of the unreconstructed material reality on stage, or of spectacle and ideology in theatre: is there a way in which, as spectators, we are inherently drawn to visions of order, especially to overpowering, monolithic, even totalitarian presentations?

Žižek is a fatalistic thinker who has much in common with Jacques Derrida – he writes that deconstruction is 'in a radical sense *commonsensical*'.[26] By this he means that deconstruction recognizes the limits imposed on human beings by the nature of the real itself, limits which define the human condition as such. This condition entails an irreconcilable contradiction between our need for a modicum of order and meaning in the world and our traumatic encounter with 'the Real in its utter, meaningless idiocy'.[27] There is an inescapable pathology about our relation of misrecognition with reality; at the very bottom the human is a 'symptom', which not even deconstruction or psychoanalysis can get us past. In our rage for order over chaos we always fantasize, taking pleasure in constructing ideological systems which, paradoxically, the more harmonious they are the more they risk totalitarianism, mass murder and holocaust: our rage for order inevitably has a totalitarian side, the 'Stalinism of language'.[28] To think, as do Deleuze and Guattari, that the Anti-Oedipus can escape this fate is naive and probably dangerous. The better task is to acknowledge, rather than attempt to escape, the antagonism at the root of human life and 'to learn to recognize it in its terrifying dimension and then, on the basis of this fundamental recognition, to try to articulate a *modus vivendi* with it'.[29] Like Blau, Žižek holds on to a faith in democracy, despite the impossibility of democracy, tied to carefulness in thinking within its illusions and paradoxes:

> The democratic attitude is always based upon a certain fetish-istic split: *I know very well* (that the democratic form is just a form spoiled by stains of 'pathological' imbalance), *but just the same* (I act as if democracy were possible). Far from indicating its fatal flaw, this split is the very source of the strength of democracy: democracy is able to take cognizance of the fact that its limit lies in itself, in its internal 'antagonism'.[30]

In his interest in totalitarianism and democracy, Žižek moves psychoanalytic study beyond a focus on the individual to an interest in the largest social and political formations.

For Žižek, as for Brecht, his project is a continuation (albeit with great modifications) of the rationalism of the Enlightenment: of all Brecht's theatre, Žižek is most drawn to the learning plays, with their difficult integrity in facing up to the inescapable paradoxes of political action.[31]

Hélène Cixous

To what extent does the view that our psychic nature is inescapable need to arrest the possibility of personal and social change? Žižek argues both that humans have a totalitarian streak and that we need struggle for democracy. As noted earlier, feminist thinkers differ as to the possibility of escaping patriarchal psychic structures. The desire to escape the patriarch within has led to various attempts to undo the oedipal limitations of theatre and psychoanalysis. For instance, the French feminist writer and theorist Hélène Cixous has written a number of plays with connections to psychoanalytic theory but which also entail a critique of the sexism that haunts traditional psychoanalysis; two of the most prominent are *Portrait of Dora* and *The Name of Oedipus*.[32] *Portrait of Dora* is an adaptation of Freud's fragment of a case history of a young woman Freud calls Dora. Freud's *Dora* is infamous, especially in feminist circles, for its intertwining of insight and blindness. In it Freud carefully unravels the biases and textual strategies of his patient while ignoring the biases and strategies that so obviously structure his own discourse: Freud, along with family and society, attempts to impose a patriarchal agenda of desire and identity on Dora which she refuses to accept as her own. In the end she breaks off her appointments with Freud, leaving the analysis and Freud's case history incomplete.

Cixous's *Dora* began as a radio play, a strictly verbal exercise like Freud's case history or the 'talking cure' of pschoanalysis. Even so, the dramatization of the work in the voices of the characters decentres Freud's controlling narration and allows Cixous to retell Dora's tale free of Freud's hegemony. In this new telling, as in most feminist readings of Dora's story, Dora is both a victim of a patriarchal system which imposes an inappropriate model onto Dora's psyche and a budding heroine who refuses to go along with her own indoctrination. With the help of director Simone Benmussa and filmmaker Marguerite Duras, Cixous turned her radio play into a multimedia theatre piece, thus stressing by theatrical means the many levels of reality and understanding that go into the making of any life and subjectivity.

After *Portrait of Dora*, Cixous wrote an opera text called *The Name of Oedipus*, adapting the Sophoclean play so central in

de gender ration
— du jour

psychoanalytic theory. The French title of the play, *Le Nom D'Oedipe*, plays upon the French homonym *nom/non* (name and no), just as Lacan does in the *'nom du père'*, the name of the father – patriarchal authority through language – which is also the 'no' of the father, the prohibition and denial that make us subjects within the patriarchal order. Like Kristeva, Cixous takes a special interest in the mother and the realm of the mother, where affirmation, excess and freedom from naming and constricted identity are possible. The play is subtitled *Song of the Forbidden Body*, aligning Jocasta with a new and forbidden embodied subjectivity, a new way of being, similar to the semiotic in Kristeva and the anti-Oedipus in Deleuze and Guattari. Each character in the play is doubled, played by both an actor and a singer, thus marking the subject, the named, the unified as in reality a place of multiple voices and identities. The play begins with an 'incantatory' overlap of voices and avoids throughout a linear development, rejecting the inevitability of tragedy and fixed oedipalized identity for a fluid and open exploration of psychic multiplicity.

2 FEMINIST AND GENDER THEORY

No theoretical approaches have had as much impact in the last twenty years as those concerned with gender and sexuality. Not surprisingly, therefore, Sue-Ellen Case, Jill Dolan and Gayle Austin have each written a book which introduces feminist theories to the study of theatre and drama.[33] In these three books, feminist theory has been applied to theatre studies more systematically than has any other area of recent theory. In light of this, the discussion of feminist theory here draws heavily on these works. In addition, Elain Aston has recently introduced feminism and theatre from a distinctly British perspective.[34]

Like much materialist theory and unlike, for instance, much deconstruction, feminist theory is directly and predominantly

Hend existential

political. Its purpose is to struggle against the oppression of women as women. This oppression, which is seen to be historically extremely common and widespread, is the result of patriarchy, the supremacy of masculine power and authority most firmly entrenched in the figure of the father (thus the inevitable relations between feminism and psychoanalytic work). Feminism, therefore, works towards the unravelling and overthrow of patriarchy.

Following the work of Judith Fetterley, feminism posits the feminist as a 'resisting reader' in the face of patriarchal cultural domination. There is a recognition that traditionally, when women have been allowed to partake of the dominant culture, they have been indoctrinated in masculine values and ways of seeing, what Fetterley calls the 'immasculation' of the woman reader.[35] Feminism attempts to create a woman reader who sees otherwise and brings a different and other perspective to bear on culture.

The point is often made that, just as there is no universal woman but only women, there is not one feminism but feminisms.[36] Although this is true of other theoretical movements as well, feminist theories often stress that feminism proceeds in a number of different directions, some of which are at odds with others. One project of feminist theory is to look critically at traditional patriarchal culture. This entails a critique of the patriarchal canon and the hegemony of male artists. Virginia Woolf, in *A Room of One's Own*, points out the difficulties and patterns of exclusion which have traditionally kept women from taking prominent positions in recognized cultural production. Of particular interest to feminist scholars of theatre is Woolf's history of a hypothetical sister of Shakespeare, Judith, with equal talent and equal interest in theatre: given the material barriers which excluded early modern women from exercising their talents in a theatrical career, Judith's story is one of frustration, seduction, abandonment and suicide.[37]

The story of Shakespeare's sister goes with a general awareness of the underrepresentation of women artists in a male
culture which takes itself as universal. If most prominent
cultural work has been given over to men, it follows that most
prominent cultural work is invested in a masculine perspective. Feminist theory searches out the patriarchal values and
ideologies that inform, sometimes in silence, sometimes in an
overtly cocksure fashion, the prominent work of the masculine
canon. Without a large number of prominent women artists
or predominantly female audiences, patriarchal culture is
seen as the exchange of cultural material – often involving
representations of women – within an exclusively male and
homosocial economy. This recognition often entails a deval-
uation or rejection of works with high canonical standing
– Shakespeare's, for instance – although feminist work also
yields complex and subtle revaluations of male texts (Ann-
Marie MacDonald's play *Goodnight Desdemona (Good Morning
Juliet)*, for instance, is a sophisticated reworking of Shakespeare
through the eyes of a main character who slowly abandons
her immasculation for a feminist perspective[38]). In this regard,
the following analysis by bell hooks of her relation with the
post-colonial theorist of pedagogy and activist Paulo Freire is
exemplary in its carefulness and consideration:

> There has never been a moment when reading Freire that I have
> not remained aware of not only the sexism of the language but
> the way he (like other progressive Third World political leaders,
> intellectuals, critical thinkers such as Fanon, Memmi, etc.)
> constructs a phallocentric paradigm of liberation – wherein
> freedom and the expression of patriarchal manhood are always
> linked as though they are one and the same. For me this is
> always a source of anguish for it represents a blind spot in the
> vision of men who have profound insight. And yet, I never wish
> to see a critique of this blind spot overshadow anyone's (and

feminists in particular) capacity to learn from these insights. This is why it is difficult for me to speak about sexism in Freire's work; it is difficult to find a language that offers a way to frame critique and yet maintain the recognition of all that is valued and respected in the work. It seems to me that the binary opposition that is so much embedded into Western thought and language makes it nearly impossible to project a complex response. Freire's sexism is indicated by the language in his early works notwithstanding that there is so much that remains liberatory. There is no need to apologize for the sexism. Freire's own model of critical pedagogy invites a critical interrogation of this flaw in his work. But critical interrogation is not the same as dismissal.[39]

Feminist theory is profoundly concerned with the cultural representation of women, sometimes as a strictly masculinist fantasy with no relation to real women, sometimes as the appropriation of women and women's bodies to masculine perspectives. Patriarchal cultural visions often reduce women to behavioural stereotypes (virgin, whore, madonna, bitch) and fetished body parts (breasts, vagina, face). Laura Mulvey discusses, in relation to classic Hollywood film, the system of representation whereby the male 'gaze', of the hero, the camera, and the audience, is imposed as the only way of seeing women.[40] Since the male gaze oppresses, silences and distorts female realities (although it cannot be true that men are always and necessarily less capable than women of representing women's reality), one task of feminism is to overturn traditional systems of representation.

The body is one sight of oppression for women; subjectivity is another. Drawing, often critically, upon psychoanalytic theory, feminism attempts to understand the ideologies which have limited women's ways of becoming subjects or agents, and to open up new patterns in which women are free to escape the confines of the subjectivity patriarchy sets up for them (related work in theatre is discussed through the example of Hélène Cixous in the first part of this chapter). Representation and subjectivity are made to reveal themselves as gendered fictions rather than natural or inevitable realities.

More than a critique of masculine culture, feminism is interested in the fostering of women's cultures. In relation to the past, this entails the rediscovery and recuperation of forgotten and overlooked work by women, not only in dominant cultural modes but also in less regarded cultural forms which were traditionally the purview of women excluded from areas of male activity. In theatre studies, feminist history uncovers closet drama, marginal genres (such as domestic melodrama[41]) and various quasi-theatrical activities. Feminist theatre history is also interested in those relatively rare women who have managed to succeed in predominantly male artistic spheres. Aphra Behn, for example, becomes both a uniquely and insightfully feminine voice in the masculine world of Restoration theatre and a partly compromised and immasculated player in that world. Anne Russell, in the introduction to a recent edition of Behn's *The Rover*, writes of 'tensions and contradictions' in the play betweeen, for instance, protofeminism and the restoration of patriarchal authority.[42] Of course, any production of the play is likely to stress one side over the other, as shown in two recent versions of *The Rover*. According to Susan Carlson, John Barton's Royal Shakespeare Company production in 1986 reduced the individuality of the female characters and rendered them in part as sexual objects; JoAnne Akalaitis's 1994 production, however, brought out the liberatory and tolerant aspects of the play:

> Both in its rearrangements of text and its enhancement of the visual, Akalaitis' production clearly demonstrates that Behn's play is an exercise in possibility, not a meting of judgment. Behn

does not condemn Angellica Bianca's free sexuality, Willmore's rapacious desire's, Hellena's naiveté, or Blunt's revenge, but she makes all of them possible.[43]

For feminism, more important than recouping work of the past is the fostering of new work by women, feminist work which would represent women otherwise than patriarchy has heretofore allowed. Here feminist theatre studies take a predominating interest in the work of contemporary women.

Feminism divides into different schools as to what a feminist culture related to women's reality would be like. Radical or cultural feminism assumes a more or less essential or universal feminine mode of being, arising from the female body and its rhythms, the feminine relation to the maternal and a specifically feminine spiritual, emotional and intellectual make up. This feminine difference is to be valued, often at the expense of most things masculine. In this light, Hélène Cixous posits an 'écriture feminine', or feminine writing, a mode of expression faithful to the rhythms and intuitiveness natural to women.[44]

Materialist feminism sees the feminine as not natural but constructed in a network with other forces, such as class and race. Women do not constitute one homogeneous group, but are often at odds with each other: the interests of a poor, black woman and those of a rich, white woman are not likely to coincide completely. Materialist feminism refuses to posit a feminine essence of which all women must partake and sees in this idea something coercive and restrictive.

The situation is complicated further by the feminist theory of women of colour, which sees white women as a hegemonic group who have designated themselves to speak for all women. Much feminism, but especially the work of women of colour, is concerned with the position from which anyone speaks and questions those who speak on behalf of others. Here is Sue-Ellen Case introducing her discussion of women of colour:

Because this description of the position and project of women of colour has been written by a white author, the discourse is necessarily distanced from the actual experiences which shape this position. The distance is not an objective distance, but one which reflects a perspective of racial and class privilege. The white author cannot write from the experience of racial oppression, or from the perspective of the ethnic community, and must thus omit a sense of the internal composition of such a community or of its interface with the dominant white culture. Moreover, within the study of feminism and theatre, this distance creates crucial problems in research and criticism.[45]

Women of colour have a different relation than white women do to the white (male) canon, to men of colour and to the hegemonic white discourse. Even more than white women, women of colour have had their perspectives and voices erased from the dominant culture, and therefore have a different struggle in asserting their perspectives and voices.[46] Black feminism has also argued that theory itself is part of an exclusionary, white discourse which does not relate to the experiences of black women.[47]

Lesbian feminism adds another element to these negotiations and brings new perspectives to gender identity, heterosexuality, the male gaze, the representation of women and the exchange of women in a patriarchal economy. At its most optimistic, lesbian theory claims that lesbian relations escape patriarchal oppression, representation and the male gaze. (Of course, not all lesbians will be positioned similarly: a poor, Asian lesbian will have different investments than a rich, white lesbian.)

Teresa de Lauretis discusses the problems faced by lesbian work and thought, which seek to assert lesbian sexual difference within the hegemonic context of masculine 'hommosexuality', whose predominating characteristic is its *in*difference to (as both an inability to see and a disregard for) whatever lies outside heterosexist norms. She writes:

lesbian writers and artists have sought variously to escape gender, to deny it, to transcend it, or perform it in excess, and to inscribe the erotic in cryptic, allegorical, realistic, camp, or other modes of representation, pursuing diverse strategies.[48]

Stressing the way that heterosexism entraps and assimilates lesbian representation, Jill Dolan has recently stressed not only the need to break representational conventions of the male gaze, but the importance of the explicit presentation of lesbian sexuality as a 'truly radical' and 'sufficiently blatant' way of transgressing and subverting the status quo:

Because gay male or lesbian sexuality is completely out of place – unimaged, unimagined, invisible – in traditional aesthetic contexts, the most transgressive act at this historical moment would be representing it to excess, in dominant and marginalized reception communities. The explicitness of pornography seems the most constructive choice for practicing cultural disruptions.[49]

In this essay, Dolan is explicitly and forcefully confronting what she calls 'hegemonic antiporn feminism',[50] which sees pornography as both painful to many women and a real threat to all – two claims Dolan treats with dismissive unkindness. She is similarly dismissive of realist representations of normalized lesbian 'lifestyles' and relationships (normatively monogamous and assimilationist) and soft-focused lesbian 'eroticism'.

Caryl Churchill and Ntozake Shange

Caryl Churchill's *Cloud Nine* does most of its feminist work in a specifically theatrical way, in the interplay between characters and actors. *Cloud Nine*, which developed out of a theatrical workshop on sexual politics, is a broadly-based attack on a number of interrelated hegemonic forces of oppression: sexism, heterosexism, racism, colonialism, classism. The first act takes place in Victorian Africa and is centred around Clive, the *pater familias* and colonial overlord, who imposes his ideals on those (women, blacks, homosexuals) around him. 'I live for Clive,' declares Betty, Clive's wife, and later, 'Clive is my society.'[51] Betty is both oppressed and incapable of imagining herself otherwise. Edward, Clive's homosexual son, Joshua, his black servant and Harry, his homosexual friend, struggle to varying degrees with similar ideological constraints. At the end of act one, Joshua, spurned by Clive, in an act of disillusion and disappointment, shoots his master.

The most striking aspect in the *mise-en-scène* of act one is the relation between actors and characters. Betty, for instance, is played by a man; Joshua is played by a white, Edward by a woman and Victoria, Clive's daughter, by a dummy. As Betty says, 'I am a man's creation as you see, / And what men want is what I want to be.'[52] Each of these characters has imposed on them a social identity which oppresses them and limits the possibility of remaking themselves in a more liberated and self-chosen way. As the actor's gendered or racial reality is distorted in his or her stage role, each character has been saddled with a role which imposes a false sense of self.

Act two takes the same characters, minus Clive, to contemporary London. Now characters are played by actors of their own sex: Betty by a woman, Edward by a man and so forth. The one exception is Cathy (the 4-year-old daughter of Lin, a friend of the now grown Victoria), who is played by a man – in the original production by the actor who played Clive in act one. In large part this rearrangement of roles entails an escape from oppression into more natural identities. As Churchill tells us, 'Betty is now played by a woman, as she gradually becomes real to herself.'[53] And yet, the play does not present us with a naive or simplistic sense of essentialized gendered identity. Edward, for instance, though now played by a man, clings to the feminine identity he sees as his own. When Gerry,

Edward's lover, says to him, 'Eddy, do stop playing the injured wife, it's not funny,' Edward responds, 'I'm not playing. It's true.'[54] Later, when he begins to explore a sexual relationship with Victoria, Edward says, 'I think I'm a lesbian'. Lin, a lesbian, struggles with the limitations that the past imposes on remaking her identity: 'I've changed who I sleep with, I can't change everything.'[55] Even Betty finds her newfound identity a struggle to get used to. She has a hard time, for instance, becoming comfortable with the act of masturbating she has so come to enjoy:

> It felt very sweet, it was a feeling from very long ago, it was very soft, just barely touching, and I felt myself gathering together more and more and I felt angry with Clive and angry with my mother and I went on and on defying them, and there was this vast feeling growing in me and all around me and they couldn't stop me and no one could stop me and I was there and coming and coming. Afterwards I thought I'd betrayed Clive. My mother would kill me. But I felt triumphant because I was a separate person from them. And I cried because I didn't want to be. But I don't cry about it any more. Sometimes I do it three times in one night and it really is great fun.

For Churchill, in the second act all the characters 'change a little for the better',[56] but this doesn't mean that they all find their essential selves, only that they are somewhat freed up to struggle and explore – as Betty says, 'if there isn't a right way to do things you have to invent one'.[57] In this light, the invocation of archetypal womanliness, though compelling, is fraught with an inevitable failure – as Victoria intones: 'Goddess of many names, oldest of the old, who walked in chaos and created life ... give us back what we were, give us the history we haven't had, make us the women we can't be.'[58]

And what about Cathy being played by a grown man, especially the man who was Clive? One way of looking at this is to see the superego which dominated in act one replaced by the id of the rambunctious child and of contemporary sexual 'liberation'. Remember also that in act one the young girl was played by a dummy: to be a young girl in the Victorian past was to be assigned a role so confining as to be lacking in basic humanity. In act two, on the other hand, the young girl is allowed a verve and presence the equal of an adult male's. Finally, by disjoining character and actor, Churchill intimates that for the pre-oedipalized child there is no inevitable and appropriate identity; she is, at least potentially, free to direct her energies in any way she can imagine.

At the end of the play, the ghost of Clive returns to haunt Betty, who confronts her earlier self from act one – not that she capitulates to the forces of the past, but these forces do remain with her, as part of her identity and her possibilities. In this moment Churchill both addresses the continuing reality of patriarchy and its phallocentric economy and refuses to be overwhelmed by them. Churchill, it has been noted, 'remains committed to the search for new representational forms, new strategies for encoding the body, new ways to organize the sex/gender relations we live in', while taking cognizance of the cultural conditions under which the new must come into being.[59]

Ntozake Shange's *for colored girls who have considered suicide / when the rainbow is enuf* is a renowned work of black feminist theatre. As such, it features a number of concerns common to black feminist theatre and feminist theatre in general. The play, or 'choreopoem', arose in a context of collective creation and collaboration and in the interchanges between those involved in poetry, dance, music and theatre. (Dance, for Shange, was especially important as an access point to her African interests.) The work was also influenced by the study of women's history:

Unearthing the mislaid, forgotten, &/or misunderstood women writers, painters, mothers, cowgirls, & union leaders of our

pasts proved to be both a supportive experience & challenge
not to let them down, not to do less than – at all costs not to
be less woman than – our mothers.[60]

The play itself interweaves music, word and dance in order
to show 'a young black girl's growing up, her triumphs
& errors, our struggle to become all that is forbidden by our
environment, all that is forfeited by our gender, all that we
have forgotten'.[61] In part this becoming entails the finding of
a language and 'the sound / of her own voice / her infinite
beauty'.[62] The play features a combination of poetry and black
vernacular which invokes an '*écriture feminine*' for women of
colour.

The black women in the play have a particular set of
relationships with black men (or with white women). On one
side there is a connection with black male leaders of the past:

TOUSSAINT L'OUVERTURE
became my secret lover at the age of 8
i entertained him in my bedroom
widda flashlight under my covers
way inta the night / we discussed strategies
how to remove white girls from my hopscotch games
& etc.[63]

In this regard, black people stand together against white
oppression, including the oppression of white girls and women.
On the other side there is the trauma of sexual abuse and rape
by which black men have oppressed black women, a trauma
which binds black women with white women against men
both black and white. The play begins with the characters,
seven women, in 'postures of distress', but by the end there is
a triumph of voice and self: 'i found god in myself / & i loved
her / i loved her fiercely.'[64] Here the play taps into a spirit-
ualism important to black culture and to feminist interest in the

goddesses of ancient matriarchies, an interest more common in radical than materialist feminism.

In contrast to the confrontational and uncompromising lesbian theatre promoted by Jill Dolan, Shange's twentieth-anniversary production of *for colored girls* in New York in 1995 stressed those aspects of the play which are softer, less alarming, comforting and nurturing. This effect was achieved in large measure by adding more music and organic movement to the production, so that the general effect was one of solace and community.[65] As open and accepting as this production was, however, a 1991 production of the play in Denver went much further. Directed by a gay white male, the production attempted to get at the 'universal aspects' of the play in order to deal with 'all kinds of oppression'. In this regard, the production featured images from the work of Robert Mapplethorpe.[66] Such a production runs the risk of effacing, or at least undermining, the particularities of black women's experience which gave rise to the play.

Queer theory

Lesbian feminist theory unites, to some extent, with gay male theory to form the new discipline of queer theory. Queer theory moves from what Eve Kosofsky Sedgwick calls a 'minoritizing' interest in homosexuality and homosexuals narrowly defined to a 'universalizing' interest in the construction of sexuality in general and its relations with power.[67] There is an echo here of Adrienne Rich's earlier notions of compulsory heterosexuality and the lesbian continuum: compulsory heterosexuality is neither natural nor universal but constructed and enforced in conjunction with other relations of power to the detriment of alternative sexual practices and identities; the lesbian continuum implies that there aren't simply lesbians on one hand and heterosexual women on the other but a broad range of practices and identities.[68] Queer theory, therefore, studies the hegemonic apparatuses and ideologies of heterosexuality and the 'epistemology of the closet', the practices whereby an oppressed homosexuality is indirectly expressed, on the one hand, and the means of reading homosexuality in all its forms within a heterosexual hegemony, including underlying patterns of sexual variance which give the lie to any idea that our culture is as straight as it likes to think it is. This study gives rise to the ubiquitous gerund 'queering' (as in, for example, 'queering the Renaissance'), describing an activity wherein alternative 'queer' practices and attitudes are found at the heart of a culture or period traditionally taken as heterosexual.

Queer theory ultimately points towards a sexuality open to varied and shifting practices and identities. In this it echoes Michel Foucault's call for 'a general economy of pleasure not based on sexual norms' and Julia Kristeva's for the relativity of each person's symbolic as well as biological existence.[69] Some sense of the openness implied in the term can be seen in the following passage:

> The term Queer is manifold; it seeks to encompass that which has been excluded, ridiculed, oppressed. Life caught in the margins. Sex yes, and sexuality, but also gender, race, class, and that which refuses easy taxonomy and suffers the fate of difference. A philosophy never fixed nor realized, but a politics of shared struggle, and a striving for community.[70]

Seen in this light, Churchill's *Cloud Nine* appears as a consumately queer play. Furthermore, left this open, queer theory and queer studies seem open to any fellow traveller who, for reasons of solidarity or opportunity, wishes to work under the rubric. This causes some unease among gays and lesbians who have long fought against a homophobic culture. Moreover, the 'postmodern' openness of queer studies has been contrasted with more historically grounded and politically focused work in traditional gay and lesbian studies.[71]

Following Foucault's *History of Sexuality*, queer theory explores the construction of sexuality in history – both hetero-sexuality and homosexuality come into being only in certain historical situations. The recent work of Jonathan Goldberg, for instance, explores modes of sexuality in the Renaissance. The early modern period of course becomes more queer than it has heretofore.[72]

Marjorie Garber's *Vested Interests: Cross-Dressing & Cultural Anxiety* explores the sexual and cultural significance of trans-vestism (a topic much favoured in recent critiques of gender) both historically and in the present.[73] In transvestism gender is related to role-playing and to such materially specific practices as putting on clothes. If clothes make the man, they also some-times make the man a woman or the woman a man.

The relation between transvestism, role-playing and gender has been fruitfully explored in the study of boy actors playing women's parts in Renaissance theatre. Was it truly a 'woman's part' when played by a boy, or does the phenomenon of boy actors strongly point out how 'women' on stage were a product of masculine imagination and fabrication? Do men kissing boys pretending to be women point to the underlying homosocial and homoerotic realities of early modern theatre? Do, rather, boys playing women highlight the artificiality and complexity of gender identity? Think of Rosalind in *As You Like It*: a boy plays a woman pretending to be a boy, and then a boy plays a woman pretending to be a boy pretending to be a woman. What actor could keep all this straight? How would such a layering of masquerade appear to an audience? Would this layering cast gender identity into a comic vertigo, or was this such an accepted convention that no one saw anything out of the ordinary? At any rate, how much different is the Shakespeare we usually get today, when 'women's parts' are routinely played by women?

Some of the possible effects that can be generated by

wedding Renaissance practices of theatrical cross-dressing with current sexual politics can be seen in Cheek by Jowl's recent production of *As You Like It*. In this version, Adam and Audrey were doubled, and Rosalind was played by a six-foot tall black man. Writing about this British production as presented in Brooklyn in 1994, Katie Laris sees it 'debunking the value of such societally-determined attributes as gender, race, and even age'. She adds, 'The ease with which these actors transform themselves and the degree to which the audience accepts these characters, compellingly illustrates how ultimately artificial such categories are.'[74]

In beginning to develop a poetics of gay male theatre, Robert Wallace calls for a 'homosexual gaze' which 'decentres the aesthetic of the heterosexual male gaze', positing gay experiences as central in a spirit of self-affirmation and assertion. At the same time, gay theatre must not turn away from marginalization as a gay experience, nor from patriarchal oppression and the self-oppression it often imposes. For Wallace, gay theatre, like feminist theatre, is drawn to disruptions of the traditionally realist masculinist gaze by resorting to self-referentiality and the exposure of theatrical illusion. Non-realist theatre also has the advantage of invoking the constructedness and not the naturalness of social norms, including those of gender and identity.[75]

Angels in America

Tony Kushner's two-part *Angels in America* (*Millenium Approaches* and *Perestroika*[76]) is one of the foremost works of recent gay male theatre. As such, it displays both a traditional 'minoritizing interest' in the lives of gay men and a 'universalizing' interest in new modes of sexuality. The minoritizing side can be seen in the standard references to icons of gay culture – *The Wizard of Oz*, Cole Porter, Blanche Dubois in *A Streetcar*

Named Desire (even the use at key moments of extravagant spectacle play into a stereotypically gay sensibility) – as well as in the focus on particularly gay experiences: one character is a former drag queen, two others suffer from AIDS (which in Kushner's plays remains a gay disease). *Angels in America* is also, however, as its subtitle states, 'A Gay Fantasia on National Themes'; as such, it sets its gay characters and interests at the heart of general concerns of religion, politics, culture and society in America. For Kushner, to be gay is not to be outside American life, but to live it through and through; and the great concerns of American life are gay as much as they are straight. *Perestroika* ends looking forward to a time, which has perhaps come, when gay men 'will be citizens'.[77] With its scenes in a fantastical Soviet Union and in a heaven that looks like San Francisco after the earthquake, *Perestroika* takes gay concerns into the international and cosmic spheres as well.

Kushner has consciously enacted a theoretical and political position in his theatre. He is a very theoretically literate playwright, taking a profound interest in such theorists as Walter Benjamin (discussed in Chapter 3), with his interest in apocalypse and utopia. He also follows in the footsteps of Caryl Churchill, whom he considers the 'greatest living, English-language playwright',[78] and takes a similar interest in the complexities and contingencies of identity. Moreover, Kusher aligns his project with the politics of groups such as Queer Nation:

> Like Queer Nation, *Angels in America* aims to subvert the distinction between the personal and the political, to refuse to be closeted, to undermine the category of the 'normal,' and to question the fixedness and stability of every sexual identity.[79]

As in much recent queer theory, *Angels in America* plays with set notions of sexual preference. The most troubling character in the two plays is Roy M. Cohn, a right-wing power broker dying of AIDS, who asserts, 'Homosexuals are men who know nobody and who nobody knows. Who have zero clout. Does this sound like me...?' 'Roy Cohn is not a homosexual,' he declares. 'Roy Cohn is a heterosexual man who fucks around with guys.'[80] As reactionary as Cohn's attitudes are, they speak to the complexities of personal, social and sexual identity. Furthermore, the angel who visits and copulates with Prior Walter, also an AIDS patient, has eight vaginas and is 'Hermaphroditically Equipped as well with a Bouquet of Phalli'.[81]

And yet the angel preaches a reactionary sermon of going back and staying put, of a return to the past, which the plays reject. 'The Great Work Begins', says Prior at the end of *Perestroika*, taking on a commitment to '*More Life*', to the remaking of America as a place free of sexual and racial oppression. *Perestroika*, writes Kushner, is essentially a comedy, but one with high stakes and a terrific amount of struggle.[82] If there is a problem with Kushner's work, it is that there is a lack of precision and clarity as to how all the themes brought forward hang together, and if the struggle and stakes are high, specifics of strategy and goal remain unclear. This lack of clarity can be taken in at least two ways. First, it may be a necessary part of the utopian instinct directed towards an unknown future: 'a teleology, not a guarantee.'[83] On the other hand, it can be taken as a symptom of the circumstances of confusion and complicity in which *Angels in America* arises; given this particular 'field of cultural production', David Savran argues, the play could hardly avoid certain ambivalences.[84]

3 READER-RESPONSE AND RECEPTION THEORY

Reader-response and reception theory, taken together, are concerned with how people other than the author or creator contribute to the meaning of a work of art. In literary matters they are concerned with the practice of making meaning on the part of a reader or readers. Widely conceived, as a general theory of the appropriation of works of art, they have connections with many theoretical approaches. Reception theory can be understood in part as a branch of phenomenology. Wolfgang Iser, for instance, is interested in the work of art, specifically literary art, as a phenomenon which manifests itself to the consciousness of the reader in the time of the act of reading.[85] The reader encounters the text in a way analogous to, if not the same as, the way we encounter the world. Hans Robert Jauss is more interested in the changing interpretations of a work of art from era to era and in this way he moves reception theory in a historical and materialist direction.[86]

Post-structuralism has also been interested in the activity of reading, most notably in Roland Barthes' distinction between the readerly and writerly text: the readerly text leads the reader along by limiting and imposing its meaning; the writerly text is open to, and encourages, the reader rewriting and recreating the text in the joy of reading.[87] Is it the text, however, which makes for a readerly or writerly reading, or is it the reader who brings an open or closed approach to whatever text? On a sociocultural and political level, Stanley Fish goes further in this direction: he relates, for instance, the ability of his students to read a list of linguistics scholars mistakenly as a seventeenth-century devotional poem. According to Fish, there are no meanings inherent in works of art except those which 'interpretive communities' in any particular era foster or allow, while disallowing and discouraging others. Power determines meaning.[88]

From a marxist perspective, Tony Bennett writes, 'Marxist criticism has assumed that every text has its politics inscribed in it, but that politics has to be made', and 'In this sense, literature is not something to be studied; it is an area to be occupied.'[89] Terry Eagleton posits the multifold task of the 'revolutionary cultural worker' as not only participation in the production of new works but also the appropriation of existing works through radical criticism and interpretation.[90] Judith Fetterley's notion of the 'resisting reader' brings reader-response within a feminist aesthetic strategy.

A historicized reception theory involves the rewriting of the significance of a text in changing circumstances. The significance of *Othello*, for instance, has changed with shifting societal attitudes toward race, as *The Taming of the Shrew* is affected by attitutes about women and *The Merchant of Venice* by attitutes towards anti-semitism. Translation studies go one step further and examine the rewriting of the text itself. Recent translation theory expands the idea of translation from its traditional, limited sense to include rewriting in all its forms (the production of a dramatic text on a stage, for instance) and what may be called the recontextualization of the work of art. Rewriting and recontextualization move from marginal and secondary activities to encompass perhaps all literary activity – any new work is a complex rewriting of the cultural objects of the past.[91] Translation so concerned relates to Derrida's notion of iterability, and it is not surprising that translation is for Derrida another area of interest. Deconstruction unsettles the stability of the original text and casts it into an open exchange with its translation, an exchange which refuses to privilege one over the other.[92] Similarly author and reader are no longer in a hierarchical relation whereby the author imparts meaning to the reader. Rather, the reader gives as much to the author as the author does to the reader. As Derrida says,

> But it would be necessary to analyze very closely the experience of hearing someone else read a text you have allegedly written or signed. All of a sudden someone puts a text right in front of you again in another context, with an intention that is both somewhat yours and not simply yours. . . . It can reconcile you

with what you've done, make you love it or hate it. There are
a thousand possibilities. Yet one thing is certain in all this
diversity, and that is that it's never the same.[93]

Paul de Man sees all allegory as a narrative about the impossibility of reading, in the sense of finding an author-imposed set of meanings. As allegories of reading, works of literature become self-reflexive or self-referential meditations on their own interpretability.[94]

Another practice in which past works are appropriated and rewritten is adaptation, which we have seen at work in Müller's *Hamletmachine*, Grotowski's *Akropolis*, Blau's *Elsinore* and *Crooked Eclipses*, the Performance Group's *Dionysus in 69*, and MacDonald's *Goodnight Desdemona*. Theatrical adaptation is particularly rich in the methods available for remaking the meaning of past works. The drama text, of course, can be altered in any number of ways: in his *Measure for Measure*, Charles Marowitz uses only the words of Shakespeare's play, but cutting and rearranging them to create a much more sinister story. In *Goodnight Desdemona*, MacDonald jumbles Shakespearean lines with pastiche of her own. Aimé Césaire's *A Tempest* uses little of Shakespeare's language. Blau's *Elsinore* mixes snippets of Hamlet with lines developed by the actors in rehearsal; his *Crooked Eclipses* works only with the lines of Shakespeare's sonnets, but cutting and pasting drastically. Moreover, there is staging to be adapted. A radical staging changes the meaning of a work even when the words remain relatively the same. An all-woman cast of *King Lear* is in some ways an adaptation. At this level of specifically theatrical adaptation, there enters into the reception and remaking of meaning in the theatre a complexity missing in strictly literary cultural practices. In theatre there is more than just words to read and remake and more than just readers who respond.

Marvin Carlson has written about the importance of the

theatre audience for semiotic theory. The complexity and openness of signification on the stage create in the audience a 'psychic polyphony' which allows individual audience members to focus their attention in any number of ways, allowing the theatrical spectator 'an unique and individual 'synchronic' reading as the play moves forward diachronically'.[95] Thus, no two spectators see exactly the same play. Similarly, theatre's 'local semiosis'[96] means that the specific arrangement of signs in any performance is unrepeatable. From night to night a performance changes in subtle or striking ways. Furthermore, the remounting of any drama text in another time and circumstance will change its semiotic content and reception even more extensively.

Susan Bennett analyses the role of the audience in theatre from a number of recent theoretical perspectives, including semiotics, post-structuralism and reader response. She concludes that the audience in traditional theatre enters into a 'social contract' in which audience members agree to be passive in their behaviour but open, eager and active in their acceptance and decoding of the signs presented to them. She calls for the 'emancipation of the spectator' evident in non-traditional and often marginalized theatre practices which allow for a more active role for the audience.[97]

Gerald Rabkin, in 'Is There a Text On this Stage?' – a title which echoes Stanley Fish's *Is There a Text in This Class?* – uses reader-response theory, as well as ideas from Barthes, Derrida and Michel Foucault, to undermine the traditional importance of the author/playwright and the written text s/he creates, and to stress the importance of open and radical interpretation often at odds with the author's intentions. Rabkin discusses the Wooster Group's *L.S.D.*, which appropriated and rewrote Arthur Miller's *The Crucible*, and the American Repertory Theatre's production of Samuel Beckett's *Endgame*, which resituated the play in an abandoned subway station. Both productions provoked lawsuits from the outraged authors, a response, it seems, little informed by an understanding of contemporary critical theory. Rabkin writes, 'The playwright's intentionality is, then, *not* irrelevant, but this intentionality is perceived within a complex matrix of interpretation', and 'we have in theatre two sets of readers – the theatre artists who traditionally "read," interpret, the written text, and the audience who read the new theatrical text created by the mediated reading'.[98]

David Mamet's *Oleanna* and Peter Brook's *Midsummer Night's Dream*

Narrowly conceived, drama texts are open to theories of reader response in the same way that works of literature are. David Mamet's controversial *Oleanna* is a case in point.[99] The play deals with the troubled relations between a male professor and his female student, relations which lead to sexual harassment charges that ruin the professor's career and provoke him at the play's end to assault the student in his office. Many have read the play as an attack on so-called political correctness, but with different levels of approval. For instance, when *Oleanna* was produced in Toronto in 1994, one male student wrote in the University of Toronto student newspaper:

> Mamet's play is a brilliantly written and scathing attack on the insidiousness of political correctness and militant feminism. . . .
>
> Militant feminists, or 'feminazis,' as one individual coined the phrase, and vitriolic mandarins of political correctness would have the masses believe that everyday life is untenable without a suffocating web of complex rules, regulations, and safety nets at every turn. They would have you believe humanity's dearest longings, that of loving and physical closeness, are fraught with ambiguity, perversity, and ulterior motives.[100]

In a less strident article, and one staying closer to the play, Bronwyn Drainie, in the *Globe and Mail*, found the play's success deeply disturbing, because the female student is presented as a 'monster', and productions in various cities have provoked audience members to shout encouragement when she is being beaten at the end of the play:

> I'm not saying *Oleanna* shouldn't be there or that you shouldn't go and see it in your community. But when you do, think very carefully about what you are watching: decide for yourself whether Mamet is presenting a fair fight or a cleverly crafted match with the conclusion long foregone.[101]

Both these readers see the play as slanted against the politically correct student, though they respond differently to this bias. In a third local review, this time of the film of *Oleanna*, which was released at the same time as the Toronto stage production, a second University of Toronto student saw the film as a disturbing representation of two equally unmeritorious characters:

> Her reactionary response to what has occurred makes Carol as unsympathetic as John. She reduces his veiled abuse to actual rape and charges him with assault. But even then, John does not see what is occurring. He is still stuck in his academic and paternal role.[102]

To what degree are the differences between these perspectives the product of differences between the theatrical production and the film, and to what degree are they the product of differences among readers?[103]

It is possible to read the play as enacting allegorically within itself the problematic of reading. Act I presents us with a first meeting, which seems more or less innocuous, which is reinterpreted in later acts as a scene of harassment. In act II, the two characters interpret the events of act I from opposed points of view; in this process the audience too is made to read its own responses in act I. Did we miss something? Was everything as innocent as it seemed? Is the student all wrong? Does she have a point? Even if the play is unfairly slanted against her, in the structure of reconsideration much of what she says forces us at least to revisit what we have seen. And is everything she suggests wrong, or are some of her accusations right? And if so, which ones, exactly? In such a state of questioning, even if we conclude that the professor was not very guilty to begin with, can we think that at the end, despite any yahoos in the audience who cheer him on, when he stands over her prostrate and beaten on the floor?

And how would our reading be affected by slight changes in staging? What if, in the first act, there was something a bit more suspicious and fawning about the professor, something a bit more sexualized about his treatment of the student? How sexual would he have to be before we could agree that his actions were problematic, unacceptable, harassment? In this regard, the first act of the play as it exists on the page is hardly more than a cipher; we only have actions we can begin to judge after we have seen a particular performance. And yet, no matter how *Oleanna* is played, hypothetical alternatives suggest themselves. *Oleanna* is a strong work for reader-response analysis not only because it polarizes an audience, not only because it provokes audience members to question their own responses, but because it opens onto the theatrical possibilities of production choices as well as audience responses as constitutive of meaning and reception.

One of the major thrusts of reader-response theory is to downplay the centrality of the author in artistic production. Theatre, however, has already long decentralized the playwright on behalf of producer, director and actors. The generation of meaning in the theatre is more complex, and involves more kinds of participants, than literary practice does. Some of this complexity is suggested, for instance, in accounts of Peter Brook's renowned and well-documented production of *A Midsummer Night's Dream*, which opened in Stratford-upon-Avon and eventually toured Europe and North America. Looking at accounts of this production opens up notions of drama text, author and theatre text to the multiplicity of agency and collaboration in the making of theatrical significance.

How is the drama text to be understood? Is it merely the words on the page? Words and intentions put there by the author? Brook believes that *A Midsummer Night's Dream*, like *King Lear*, or *Coriolanus*, is a masterpiece, an 'absolutely perfect play' which can only be reduced by textual amendment.[104] He felt no need to change a word. David Selbourne, who watched the rehearsals for the Stratford production, noted this 'fidelity to the text-as-written', in which the text was 'inviolable' and there was 'no question . . . of additions or subtractions, cuts or alterations to the writ of Shakespeare'.[105]

What becomes apparent, however, is that merely repeating the proper words does not guarantee a fidelity to the 'original meaning'. Selbourne becomes bemused that Brook attributes to the words of the text 'near-unfathomable depths'; he complains that Brook makes more of Shakespeare's text than is there, that Brook tries 'to induce responses which the text does not yield', that Brook continually misreads the text – ultimately, that Brook shows a reverence for the written coupled with a rejection of the writer.[106]

For Selbourne, fidelity to the words of the text is not enough; there must be fidelity to the sense of those words, and that sense is to be determined by authorial intention. He speaks of 'the playwright's truth in the last instance', of 'Shakespeare who conceived the whole in his imagination', of truth 'contained only in the mind of Shakespeare'; he identifies with 'the author' and wonders what Shakespeare would think 'if he rose from his tomb down the lane'.[107] For Brook, however,

Shakespeare is taken to be quite a different phenomenon, or set of phenomena. On the one hand Shakespeare is what has traditionally come to be associated with the name, a code word in each country for a set of values and expectations.[108] In Brook's England Shakespeare is the linchpin of the nineteenth-century Victorian tradition which comes down to him as 'the deadly theatre' with its admonition to 'Play what is written'.[109] But this nineteenth-century fidelity to the text is a bore and gives rise in Brook only to the desire to 'fuck Shakespeare'.[110] This Victorian bore, however, is not the real Shakespeare. The real Shakespeare isn't a bore. Nor is he a Victorian. He is an Elizabethan, and Elizabethan England was almost a total antithesis to Victorian England.[111] Elizabethan England was harsh, 'the violence, the passion, and the excitement of the stinking crowds, the feuds, the intrigues', like Eastern Europe in our own day, and so the real Shakespeare, as Jan Kott says, is our contemporary.[112] Rather, to be more precise, we are a strange cross of the Victorian and the Elizabethan, and while the Shakespeare of *Timon of Athens* is our contemporary, the Shakespeare of *Othello* is not.[113]

Ultimately, Brook is not really interested in Shakespeare the author any more than in Shakespeare's words: 'what passed through this man called Shakespeare . . . is quite different from any other author's work'; 'it's something which actually resembles reality'; 'it is the thing itself'.[114] Shakespeare is a 'creator', and his words are a set of codes for 'vibrations and impulses'.[115] Shakespeare is the 'miracle of Shakespeare', and it is not his method which interests us, it is 'the Shakespearean ambition'.[116] Brook, then, is not trying to be faithful to Shakespeare or Shakespeare's words, but to something he takes to be more originary: 'The text is not the play. Only a small part. Words change or say different things in another time and place. The director has to go beneath them and find the author's true intent.'[117] The author's intent, behind the words, is to recreate processes and rhythms of thought, preverbal impulses, 'the life behind the text', in the case of *A Midsummer Night's Dream*, to recreate magic.[118] Shakespeare's *'mots rayonnants'* play a part in this recreation, but 'all the printed word can tell us is what was written on paper, not how it was once brought to life'.[119] Sometimes the words are only approximations; sometimes they interfere with feeling.[120]

Selbourne quotes Hazlitt who said that all that is finest in *A Midsummer Night's Dream* is lost in the representation; Brook, on the other hand, says that 'the only way to find the true path to the speaking of a word is through a process that parallels the original creative one'.[121] Drama text gives way to theatre text. This will yield to us the 'secret play' that can only be discovered in rehearsals.[122] Yet Brook is just as dismissive of faithful historical reconstruction as he is of the deadly theatre: reconstruction is guess work and only of antiquarian interest.[123] The only way to recreate Shakespeare's magic is by contemporary theatrical means. Somewhat xenophobically, Selbourne notes these 'alien' tools whenever they arise: 'imported' Japanese theatre; Chinese circus; Japanese wrestlers; Pacific island ritual; Grand Guignol and Kurasawa; 'Grotow-skian effect'; 'Oz not Arden'.[124] We can note others: African ritual and music; jazz or rock performance; Vedic chant; Persian folk plays; Indian theatre.[125]

What we see, then, is a complex play of fidelity and infidelity: a fidelity to the words of the text is matched by an infidelity to Shakespeare's intended meaning; a fidelity to Shakespeare's ambition is matched by an infidelity to his theatrical method. An ultimate fidelity to life and magic is not a fidelity to Shakespeare, but in sympathy with Shakespeare's own fidelity to these concerns.

If our interest is now in the theatre text, we still must face the particulars and differences that arise in different performances even of the same production. Let us set aside the complex social and cultural materiality of the theatrical event, not attempting to define and reconstruct all those elements that would go into a full account of a theatrical production: the text, the multiple borrowings from world theatre, the actors in all their specificity, their delivery and movement, costumes, makeup, the set design, the lighting, the auditorium, ticket prices, the exact composition of the audience and the specificity of each individual member, the socio-political organization of the theatre company, the entire *mundus theatri*. Let us keep the question on a more general level. Loney's acting edition, for instance, is 'an American adaptation, based point-by-point on the prompt-book of the World Tour version'. It is 'perhaps the most definitive because it represents the refinements and simplifications which the production achieved in the Paris rehearsals for the tour and the later modifications introduced as the show travelled to such cities as Budapest, Helsinki, and Los Angeles'.[126] Are we to believe that only those who saw the world tour version towards the end of its run were privy to the 'definitive' production? Selbourne's book, on the other hand, ends with the last dress rehearsal before the opening night of the first Stratford production. His is an account of rehearsals. The production he talks about is not definitive, but constantly changing.

To ignore the rehearsal process would be to ignore an essential aspect of the production. The specificity of Brook's rehearsal process is what sets his work apart from the deadly theatre:

> In a living theatre, we would each day approach the rehearsal putting yesterday's discoveries to the test, ready to believe that the true play has once again escaped us. But the Deadly Theatre approaches the classics from the viewpoint that somewhere, someone has found out and defined how the play should be done.[127]

In rehearsal things don't stay the same; things are erased; those involved change from day to day and moment to moment.[128] Rehearsals are performances in their own right, with their own strange logic;[129] one day the actors 'wreck the entire studio':

> Anyone watching the play that morning would have found it unrecognizable and yet those of us who had participated in the chaos sensed that we had been in contact with elements of the play that no amount of discussion or carefully plotted 'production' could have revealed.[130]

If rehearsals are performances, performances must retain the quality of rehearsals: 'Creation and exploration need not and, in fact, must not stop on the last day of rehearsal'; 'theatre is always a self-destructive act and is always written on the wind'.[131] The 'endlessly moving, endlessly changing' nature of Shakespeare's material is best served by a production in which there is 'no definitive moment of public realization'.[132] Every performance, like every rehearsal, produces 'another truth': sometimes certain lines take on a meaning only for the nonce; sometimes an accident happens which will never happen again – a black dog wanders across the stage, a tray of candles causes a fire.[133] There are multiple possibilities in the so-called definitive prompt book itself: 'Puck spins plate, drops it to Obe[ron], who spins it on his own rod – if he catches it. If he drops it, a Fairy passes a spinning plate to him from SR slot.'[134] A rehearsal, a performance at the Midland Arts Centre, the 'full-scale experience' of opening night, the simplified versions of the world tour, none are definitive, 'but quite simply "other"'.[135]

Kenneth McClellan, in his snide and reactionary book, *Whatever Happened To Shakespeare?* argues that it's not 'Brook's *Midsummer Night's Dream*', 'it's Shakespeare's *Midsummer Night's Dream*'.[136] Selbourne begins his book with the same opposition: 'Will this be Brook's Dream, or Shakespeare's?'[137]

But this narrow opposition between author and director gives way in his account to a fuller understanding of theatrical agency: Brook runs up against the limitations of his actors, who possibly can only play conventional Shakespeare; after a certain point the play is in their hands, not Brook's; eventually the technicians take charge, and the setting, not the text, imposes a structure of feeling on the actors – 'If the preverbal comes before the verbal, does place come before both of them?'[138] Brook as director, like Derrida as author, is faced with his work coming back to him in almost unrecognizable form:

> Seeing a first public performance of a play one has directed is a strange experience. Only a day before, one sat at a run-through and was completely convinced that a certain actor was playing well, that a certain scene was interesting, a movement graceful, a passage full of clear and necessary meaning. Now surrounded by an audience part of oneself is responding like this audience, so it is oneself who is saying 'I'm bored,' 'he's said that already,' 'if she moves once more in that affected way I'll go mad' and even 'I don't understand what they're trying to say.'[139]

In performance the audience becomes the true master of the situation, and every audience is different: children are disillusioning; the Stratford audience conventionalizes; the Los Angeles audience doesn't get it, while the students of San Francisco do.[140] Finally, Loney's acting edition, with its long list of contributors, ends with three blank pages for 'director's notes': new actors, technicians and audiences await the next Peter Brook.

3

WORLD AND THEATRE

Materialist, postmodern and post-colonial theory

A performance text is a transmission tuned to a highly specific wavelength and a specific set of atmospheric conditions.[1]

> You sit and watch the stage
> Your back is turned –
> To what?
>
> The firing squad
> Shoots in the back of the neck
> Whole nations have been caught
> Looking the wrong way
>
> I want to remind you
> Of what you forgot to see
> On the way here[2]

In the first two chapters of this book, I have for the most part set aside the question of the relation of theatre to the broad social and political world in order to focus on the theatrical event in itself and then on the human subjects and agents at work in the theatrical event. But of course theatre happens in a larger context. Indeed, with its need for a public place, for physical resources, workers and an audience, theatre is more complexly and intimately intertwined with the outside world than many literary and other artistic activities. Moreover, changes in the world are bound to produce changes in theatrical production. Any well-rounded theory of the theatre, therefore, must take account of how theatre relates to the forces of the outside world.

As in the previous chapters, here I have chosen to focus on only three theoretical approaches. All of the theories discussed in the first two chapters make some contribution to understanding the place of theatre in the world. Feminism, for instance, is a profoundly political and social mode of understanding: women become gendered and oppressed by a patriarchal system at work everywhere in the world around us. But even deconstruction, in the hands of Derrida, has been brought to bear on such issues as apartheid and nuclear apocalypse. Nonetheless, I have chosen to focus here on materialist theory, postmodernism and post-colonialism.

Although materialist theory has arisen historically in the context of western capitalism, and although it has traditionally affirmed a marxist emphasis on the dominance of economic factors over other social and political forces, materialism widely conceived is a general historical theory arguably applicable to any time and place. This is not true of postmodernism and post-colonialism, which attempt to account for a narrower range of historical situations. For both postmodernism and post-colonialism, however, the period accounted for includes that of our present world, and therefore they are both particularly relevant for an introduction to the relations between world and theatre. Also, there are a number of overlapping concerns between the three theoretical fields: the marxist theorist Fredric Jameson, for instance, has written extensively on postmodernism, and Karl Marx ends the first volume of *Capital* with a chapter on the place of colonization in the development of capitalism.

1 MATERIALIST THEORY

It has been claimed on occasion that Paul de Man is a materialist thinker, inasmuch as his theory of intractable metaphoricity posits language outside idealist notions of intention and makes of it an independent (or material) force in human existence, history and exchange. Such a claim, however, radically misconstrues the basic principles of materialist thought. When Marx writes in the first volume of *Capital* that the history of capitalist expropriation 'is written in the annals of mankind in letters of blood and fire',[3] he is not just speaking metaphorically – although he is doing so – nor would a materialist think that these words circulate in a linguistic sphere without connection to the real. 'Letters of blood and fire' implies that language takes place in a wider range of human material concerns which give to words their meaning and import. A basic task of materialist theory is to understand the elaborate relations between language, literature and art, on the one hand, and society, history and the material world, on the other.

In traditional marxist materialism, culture is thought of as a superstructure dependent upon a socioeconomic base. The base/superstructure model tends towards a reductionism in which culture is more or less completely determined by economics and art is most often a direct reflection of economic conditions. The character of the base changes historically through variations in the mode of production (the structure of economic relations in any society), and much marxist literary criticism is concerned with understanding the relations between economics and literature in a specific time and place: N. N. Feltes, for example, has studied the modes of production of novels in Victorian England and the effect that modes of production have on the structure and content of those novels.[4]

Much marxist literary criticism, and much marxist theory, escapes the reductionism threatened by the base/superstructure model. Louis Althusser, for instance, argues that the relations between economics and culture are 'overdetermined', that is, subject to the influence of any number of historical forces not narrowly economic. Althusser sees cultural activity as one of many 'ideological state apparatuses', systems whereby people are made to submit to capitalist activity not through force and coercion (that is the sphere of the army and the police) but through 'interpellation', whereby people are brought to identify with the roles capitalism needs them to play.[5] 'Ideology' – like difference and other, an extremely resonant word in recent theory – is the imposition and enactment of this identification. Althusser borrows from Lacan the notion of the subject, but for Althusser the subject comes into being in ideology, economics and politics, rather than in language and sexual identification. For Althusser, however, art is not strictly ideological, but provides a kind of distance and insight that ideology obfuscates. Marxism is a science, according to Althusser, and provides a clear understanding of the reality of capitalism. Art does not provide scientific understanding, but it does expose the tensions and complexities that ideology tries to keep us from seeing. Pierre Macherey has attempted to systematize the understanding of how the internal tensions in a work of art expose the reality that underlies ideology.[6]

Raymond Williams complicates the relations between socioeconomics and literature in a different way. In place of monolithic capitalist forces of production, he introduces the tripartite idea of the 'dominant', the 'residual', and the 'emergent'.[7] The dominant are those hegemonic forces (of capitalism, in our world) which are most strong at any moment of history; the residual are those once strong forces associated with the past which are now weakened yet still capable of influence; the emergent are forces in ascendance which have not yet come into full strength. In any era the dominant forces exert the most influence; residual and emergent forces, however, can also have effects. A work of literature can combine elements of all three forces, thereby rendering complex and even relatively autonomous its relations with the socioeconomic order.

In *The Political Unconscious* Fredric Jameson redraws the base/superstructure model in such a way as to equalize cultural and economic forces as determinants in the mode of production.[8] Theodor Adorno sees in modern art not a reflection of capitalist oppression but more or less unfettered works of reason and enlightenment which, especially in their formal liberations, point beyond the blinkers of capitalism.[9]

Despite these complications, much marxist theory falls back ultimately on the determinant power of the economic. Althusser's overdetermination is tied to his sense of the economic as determinant 'in the last instance', although the last instance 'never comes';[10] Jameson's redrawing of cultural and economic forces leaves the economic still 'privileged'. Jameson also holds on to the notion of 'totality', which implies a coherence and unity to any social order, no matter how complex and qualified. Some materialist thinkers have tried to posit a materialism without a centre, as in the work of Chantal Mouffe and Ernesto Laclau, who add gender and race to class as determinant considerations.[11] Similarly, cultural materialism, as practised in such works as Jonathan Dollimore and Alan Sinfield's *Political Shakespeare*, opens materialism onto a more heterogeneous, *ad hoc*, and non-systematized understanding of the interplay of cultural, economic and social forces.[12] Terry Eagleton's stridently marxist work has moved to a more flexible materialism, as in his relatively recent *Ideology: An Introduction*, which is less systematizing than exploratory.[13] In the United States, new historicism, associated most strongly with Stephen Greenblatt, is a materialist movement inasmuch as it seeks to find broad cultural connections between historical situations and particular works of art that arise in those situations, but its theoretical and practical connections with marxism and marxist politics are much more attenuated than in most materialist theory.

Two other materialist theorists worthy of special attention are Walter Benjamin and Michel Foucault. Benjamin posits the 'Now of recognizability', the historically limited perspective from which anyone must perceive the world, especially the past.[14] Partly due to a perspective defined by his marxist understanding, Benjamin sees art, which has traditionally been hallowed by an 'aura' of beauty and spirit which privileges it and separates it from the world at large, in a new light:

> Whoever has emerged victorious participates to this day in the triumphal procession in which the present rulers step over those who are lying prostrate. According to traditional practice, the spoils are carried along in the procession. They are called cultural treasures, and a historical materialist views them with cautious detachment. For without exception the cultural treasures he surveys have an origin which he cannot contemplate without horror. They owe their existence not only to the efforts of the great minds and talents who have created them, but also to the anonymous toil of their contemporaries. There is no document of civilization which is not at the same time a document of barbarism.[15]

Benjamin's work is infused with a messianic faith in a utopian moment when 'one single catastrophe which keeps piling wreckage upon wreckage' gives way to a leap into the 'free heavens' of history.

Michel Foucault offers historical materialist alternatives to both Marx and Freud. Much of Foucault's work traces the effects of the discursive regimens of various scientific disciplines at certain times in history on the production and limitation of knowledge through procedural practices and systems of exclusion. Like Derrida and de Man, Foucault undermines the belief in science and reason as truth – truth is what is made or allowed to seem true. Foucault moves in his work from the study of discursive formations (scientific or medical discourse, for instance) to the study of apparatuses – discursive and extradiscursive systems and institutions (prisons, hospitals) through which power is enacted. For Foucault, these apparatuses, more than economics and modes of production, are what constitute human social patterns. These apparatuses are also responsible for enacting human subjectivity. Here Foucault posits an etiology of the subject different from those of both Freud and Althusser. In *The History of Sexuality*, Foucault takes issue with Freud's sense of human sexuality as repressed: for Foucault, society rather fosters and channels sexuality, which only exists as instituted by social apparatuses.[16] In place of Freud's psychic topography, Foucault offers a theory of the human as a conglomerate of sub-individuals, each enacted by different aspects and apparatuses of power.[17] Behind this socially activated set of sub-individuals lies nothing, perhaps, and 'man' as thought of in the west is historically no more than a face drawn in the sand to be washed away by the sea.[18]

As a practice of studying the relations between a society and its theatre, materialist theory is potentially useful for the understanding of any historical situation and could seek to address the effect of a slave economy and the cloistering of women in the household on the theatre of ancient Athens, as well as the effect of high commodification on recent musical theatre, such as Andrew Lloyd Webber's *Phantom of the Opera* or the Disney Corporation's *Beauty and the Beast*, whereby theatre becomes more economically and technically endowed and more profitable and yet more precarious and directly susceptible to market forces than ever before – a theatre that sells out in a number of senses.

Materialism and Shakespeare

One of the most accomplished studies of the relationship between a particular theatre and its historical situation is Walter Cohen's *Drama of a Nation: Public Theater in Renaissance England and Spain*. Cohen finds the pre-conditions for Renaissance public theatre in the emerging capitalism of early modern Europe, which made possible everything from the economics and structures of the theatre companies to the prevalence and function of professional dramatists. Cohen also traces the influence of class relations and attitudes on particular genres: romantic comedy, for instance (*As You Like It* or *The Merchant of Venice*), arises in the tensions between the aristocracy and the up-and-coming bourgeoisie.[19] Finally, Cohen traces the economic and social forces that led to the demise of the public theatre and the birth of more elitist and exclusive theatres throughout the seventeenth century.

Looking at Shakespeare in a contemporary setting, Robert Wallace and Richard Paul Knowles have done materialist studies of Canada's Stratford Festival. In a study of alternative and marginal theatre in Canada, Wallace discusses in passing the conditions of production at Stratford. He notes the effect of government arts grants to the festival: such grants to Stratford profoundly limit the money available to smaller, more experimental and indigenous theatres, even while shrinking grants to Stratford itself mean the festival must rely more and more on box-office success for its survival. Needing to draw large crowds, Stratford has been forced to rely on Broadway and West-End style musicals, to appeal as much to American tourists from neighbouring states as to the people of Ontario and Canada, and to stick to a formula of proven success and low risk accessibility, often at the expense of its original mandate to produce serious Shakespearean theatre.[20]

In work more narrowly focused on the festival, Knowles lays out Stratford's shifting history, from 'the founding itself . . . a delayed colonial celebration of a 19th-century brand of imperialist British nationhood (one that allows Canada's national theatre to be dedicated to the plays of *the* canonical British writer)', to 'the current "multinationalist" moment, which extends from the early 80s to the present, in the context of free trade, "globalization," and intercultural tourism'.[21] In a review of the 1993 season, Knowles outlines his materialist suppositions:

> No production of Shakespeare can be reviewed outside of its material context. . . . At Stratford, Ontario, in 1993, where even more than at most theaters the institutional context tends to function with remarkable directness as an Ideological State Apparatus, funded by government and corporate grants, and catering to an audience it presents as monolithic, the production of Shakespeare is necessarily the reproduction of a complex and shifting but nevertheless conservative, affirmative culture.[22]

In other words, Knowles argues that the economic situation of the festival, its corporate sponsors, the corporate structure of the festival company itself, its high ticket prices and reliance upon well-off, older, often American tourists, means that the festival is bound to present productions attuned to the dominant corporate-capitalist ideology. In Benjamin's terms, a Stratford production is a document of barbarism.

Such readings have the advantage of a straightforward logic and groundedness, but they run the risk of downplaying the intangibles and undecidables of literature and culture. For instance, in a number of plays – in the epilogue of *A Midsummer Night's Dream* and in the choruses of *Henry V* and *The Winter's Tale* – Shakespeare addresses his audience as 'gentles'. Such a tradition continues in our own day when an audience is addressed as 'ladies and gentlemen'. Most of us are not ladies and gentlemen, at least not in the sense of belonging to a certain privileged class. In our day, such class associations have been largely lost, and 'ladies and gentlemen' is more or less a term of mild flattery intimating that we are a polite and civilized group. In Shakespeare's day, the class associations of a term like 'gentles' was much stronger, and a large portion of the audience were decidedly not members of the class that could legitimately be called 'gentles'. Certainly it is important to realize this, and to note the discrepancy between this form of address and the composition of the actual audience. But what does it mean? Are the plays symbolically recognizing only part of the audience to the exclusion of others? Do they rather level the audience by raising all to the same social status? Do they merely flatter in a way that no one present would really take seriously? *A Midsummer Night's Dream*, it is believed, was first presented at an aristocratic wedding. Was 'gentles', therefore, an accurate and exclusionary description of its initial audience? What of the other two plays, which have their origin in the public theatre? And what of *A Midsummer Night's Dream* when later presented to a heterogeneous public audience? Perhaps there are no simple and concrete answers to our questions, and whatever effect was intended or achieved is not one we can easily identify. We are left in the realm of perspective and conjecture.

Similar problems confront us if we seek to tie the representations of complex theatrical and dramatic works to historical reality. For instance, much recent English social history tells us that the family in early modern England was an institution of affection and care. *The Winter's Tale* is an early modern play which represents the life of a family. Its first half is a nightmarish depiction of jealousy, paranoia and cruelty; its second half presents a fanciful recovery of lost loved ones. Do either of these aspects of the play relate to the family as historians present it? If not, why not? If so, how? Is it possible to make both parts of the play, seemingly diametrically opposed, relate to the same history? And what do we think when we realize that some social historians present, in contrast, a much bleaker account of the early modern family? Materialist criticism will seem jejune and mechanistic if it underplays the provisionality and discontinuities of the relations between culture and society.

In his *Theses on Feuerbach*, Marx declares that the point is not merely to interpret the world but to change it. Materialist analysis of theatre is concerned not only with positioning theatre as a consequence of its place in history but also with seeing how theatre can affect the world. Artaud calls for a theatre which would have as direct an effect on society as the plague, but theatre is rarely so bluntly powerful. Stories of plays changing the course of history are woefully rare: the Earl of Essex staged the deposition of the king in *Richard II* to stir up support when he rose against Elizabeth, but the insurrection failed anyway. Those who study the political force of theatre have to look for more subtle modes of influence.

In *Radical Tragedy*, Jonathan Dollimore discusses the political force of theatre in early modern England. Treating the plays mainly as intellectual drama, he sees the tragedies of Shakespeare and his contemporaries as undermining and interrogating the ideology and institutions of religion and state in a way that ultimately contributes to the outbreak of civil war and the overthrow of monarchy in the 1640s.[23] Thus, the drama of the period not only articulates ideological crisis but also precipitates it.[24] *King Lear*, for instance, demonstrates to the audience how the so-called 'laws of human kindness operate in the service of property, contractual, and power relations'[25] and presents ideas closely related to those in radical pamphlets of the civil war period.

Dollimore is a cultural materialist, writing in a British tradition of intellectual activism, and for strategic reasons over and above scholarly ones he perhaps overemphasizes the potential for culture to act forcefully and decisively on political and social issues. In the United States, cultural materialism has been less influential than new historicism, spearheaded by Stephen Greenblatt.[26] New historicism has been strongly influenced by the work of Foucault on the ways that institutions of power both foster and channel such forces as sexuality, madness, illness and crime (think of Renaissance theatre as one of Foucault's 'apparatuses'). This has given rise to the twin concepts of subversion and containment: the state needs to foster insurrection in order to exercise its powers of response; representations of radical and subversive activity and thought on the stage, especially when ultimately overcome, contribute to the legitimacy and authority of the powers that be. Moreover, monarchical power in the early modern period worked in part by representational display akin to theatre, further drawing the two into close complicity. Renaissance drama and theatre, from this perspective, contribute inescapably to the regeneration of the state. Foucault, however, does not preach only defeatism in the face of power – he himself was a committed activist in areas such as prison reform; nor is there any essential reason why subversion must always be coupled with containment – and such a coupling makes the world, of the Renaissance or the late twentieth century, seem more absolutist and fated than it necessarily is.

Earlier, I made mention of Terry Eagleton's discussion of the task of the 'revolutionary cultural worker' as, in part, the appropriation of works of art through radical interpretation.

Sometimes this manifests itself in seeing, as Benjamin declares, the barbarism in cultural treasures; other times it comes in seeing the revolutionary import in seemingly conservative or reactionary works. An example of this second approach can be seen in Bertolt Brecht's materialist analysis of the opening scene of *Coriolanus*. Brecht is willing to rewrite Shakespeare, if necessary, but in this case he sets his troupe the narrower task of analysing without adding to or changing Shakespeare's text, and bringing out aspects of interpretation by staging and production alone.[27] In contrast to the 'bourgeois theatre', which focuses all its attention on the hero, and thereby aligns itself with the patricians' cause,[28] Brecht is explicitly interested in examining the class struggle in the opening scene from the plebeians' situation: 'we want to find out as much about the plebeians as we can.'[29] Brecht reads such an interest in Shakespeare's text itself.

For Brecht, Shakespeare's play is 'splendidly realistic'.[30] The opening scene demonstrates 'how hard it is for the oppressed to become united', and teaches, *inter alia*, 'That the position of the oppressed classes can be strengthened by the threat of war and weakened by its outbreak'.[31] The play is rich in conflict and contradiction, and because it offers no easy solutions it 'gives rise to discomfort'; in this way it offers 'first-hand experience of dialectics'.[32]

The point of producing the scene becomes to 'strengthen' these aspects of Shakespeare's text. For example, by making the weapons of the plebeians makeshift and yet ingenious and effective, and by contrasting them with the professional soldiers under patrician control, we can see that the plebeians are a force to be reckoned with and yet in a precarious position in their class struggle.[33] At the end of the scene, when an external threat of war has united – but only partly and temporarily – the classes of Rome, it is important to show the limits of this union in the way the members of the two classes interact.[34]

For Brecht there is great revolutionary potential in reason and understanding, and a careful analysis of Shakespeare furthers our understanding: 'The wealth of events in a single short scene. Compare today's plays with their poverty of content!'[35] He notes, 'within these complex events on a particular morning in Rome . . . there is much that a sharp eye can pick out. And certainly if you can find clues to these events, then all power to the audience!'[36]

As an alternative to questioning or subverting the status quo, cultural forms can also take on a utopian or romance function, presenting a vision of a different social order preferable to our own. As a public space, theatre functions as what the anthropologist Victor Turner calls the liminoid, a place set apart for the process of transformation, or what Foucault calls heterotopia, a quasi-public space which functions to reflect, expose, invert, support or compensate for the outside world.[37] Thematically, there is in many of Shakespeare's plays the 'green world', a place of retreat from the dominant social order. In the romances, the possibility of open and endless transformation – 'storm perpetual' or 'unpath'd waters, undream'd shores' in The Winter's Tale – is suggested, only to be foreclosed by happy return at the end of the play.

Many materialist theorists are wary of the utopian mode in culture. In a recent study of the English Romantics, the deconstructionist-marxist Forest Pyle argues that the idea of a transformed future is always unproductively limited by imaginative efforts to represent it, and that it is better to leave it as an absence or gap open to unforeseeable conditions to come.[38] Similarly, Jameson argues that, although the utopian drive is inherent in culture and is not unconnected to the revolutionary drive, it often takes a nostalgic or reactionary form, finding solutions in unfortunate places.[39] Cohen, however, stands by the importance of the romantic drive in theatre and society:

Indeed, Marxism has always wagered that in the long run human history would have, or at least could have, the structure of romance. Precisely in its utopianism, then, romance may offer a legitimate vision not of the prehistory lived in class society, but of that authentic history that may someday succeed it.[40]

Similarly, the theorist of pedagogy Paulo Freire, discussed more fully elsewhere in this chapter, writes:

On the other hand – while I certainly cannot ignore hopeless-ness as a concrete entity, nor turn a blind eye to the historical, economic, and social reasons that explain that hopelessness – I do not understand human existence, and the struggle needed to improve it, apart from hope and dream.[41]

If the utopian drive is important – as is, at the same time, a sense of actuality and possibility – then the task is, in the phrase of Raymond Williams, 'to make hope practical, rather than despair convincing'.[42]

Some of the problems and tensions around the adequacy of any utopian model can be seen in Northrop Frye's regard for *The Tempest*. For Frye, romance is the most profound literary form, and *The Tempest* is one of our most important visions of an ideal community. Because of Frye's faith in western liberal democracy, romance for him is merely a movement forward – albeit a giant leap forward – from the way things are in the modern world. Many materialist thinkers do not have such faith in the western tradition. Post-colonial writers, for instance (as discussed in the final part of this chapter), have seen in *The Tempest* not a vision of an ideal society but rather a vision of imperialist practice and ideology. In an early introduction, Frye denies the relevance of colonialism for an understanding of *The Tempest*:

It is a little puzzling why New World imagery should be so prominent in *The Tempest*, which really has nothing to do with the new world, beyond Ariel's reference to the 'still-vexed Bermoothes' and a general, if vague, resemblance between the relation of Caliban to the other characters and that of the American Indians to the colonizers and drunken sailors who came to exterminate and enslave them.[43]

Later, Frye is able to see the relation between imperialism and the play, but only by turning away from the extermination and enslavement he has already recognized. Frye connects the play to the idealized imperialist vision of Samuel Daniel in *Musophilus*, 'where the poet speaks of extending English into unknown parts of the world'. Frye adds, 'Note that Daniel is talking about language, not military conquest: the power of art, not arms'.[44] But Shakespeare's play is filled with much more force and cruelty than this implies. It may be that any utopian expression is bound to trip up somewhere along the line; *The Tempest* itself recognizes this in the utopian vision of Gonzalo, the end of which contradicts the beginning. Utopian visions are to be taken with a grain of salt, but whether they should be avoided altogether is another question.

A currently busy area of materialist work is what is called 'cultural studies', which began at Birmingham University in Great Britain in the 1950s and has since arisen in permutated forms in the United States, Canada, Australia and parts of Africa.[45] Although it is by definition and practice an open and provisional activity, cultural studies has shown certain characteristics which have remained more or less important in its wanderings. First and foremost, for many, cultural studies is not merely academic but politically engaged (although this is the aspect that has been lost the most, especially in the United States). The politics of cultural studies has moved from a narrowly marxist focus to an expansive inclusion of new issues such as gender and race. Connected with political engagement, cultural studies has been predominantly interested in contemporary popular culture and struggle. As a consequence, in its travels cultural studies has embraced the local conditions of culture, so that each locale must reinvent the particulars of cultural studies, what it is about and what it sets out to accomplish.[46]

Cultural studies tends to focus on popular culture in two senses: mass culture and the marginal, alternative forms of activity of the 'people' in a socialist sense. In theatre studies, this might entail, on the one hand, *The Phantom of the Opera*, and on the other, various alternative theatrical collectives at work in a particular locale. The studies of Knowles or Wallace of Stratford or queer theatre could be taken as instances of localized cultural studies, specifically Canadian, as it relates to theatre.

The cover of a recent cultural theory reader features images of the *Mona Lisa* used in an advertisement for dairy cream.[47] Cultural studies is interested in high western culture predominantly in the ways it is appropriated in current contexts. Much recent study of Shakespeare – in which the visual trope of reconfiguring Shakespeare's picture is commonplace – could be taken in this regard as cultural studies. Gary Taylor, for instance, writes of 'Shakesperotics' as 'everything a society does in the name . . . of Shakespeare', while Graham Holderness, in *The Shakespeare Myth*, writes, 'For every particular present, Shakespeare is, here, now, always, what is currently being made of him'.[48] Think of t-shirts, coffee mugs, ads for computer software, national theatres, tourist-town economies, school systems and radical theatrical adaptations. Canadian cultural studies will be interested in Shakespeare inasmuch as his work takes root in a specifically Canadian institution such as Stratford, or the writing of Northrop Frye, or the feminist collective Nightwood Theatre and its production of Ann-Marie MacDonald's *Goodnight Desdemona*.

Although there are ways in which cultural studies can take

an interest in something like Shakespeare or the *Mona Lisa*, works from the past are by no means the central focus of cultural studies work. The recent and compendious collection *Cultural Studies* features only one article of thirty-nine on material not explicitly contemporary.[49] That this article is on Shakespeare is less telling than that it stands alone, isolated and somewhat forlorn. For cultural studies, Shakespeare and the past are just not that important.

2 POSTMODERN THEORY

Postmodern theory and theories of the postmodern differ depending on what they understand the postmodern to be. For Jean-François Lyotard and Gianni Vattimo, postmodernism is a way of thinking. In *The Postmodern Condition*, Lyotard argues that postmodernism entails the failure of all master narratives, which might allow for a total and unified understanding of the world. In place of master narratives, Lyotard posits micronarratives and language games, performability over truth, pluricity over unity, exchange over legitimation.[50] For Vattimo, postmodern thinking entails 'weak thought', provisional and ongoing, without a foundation in universal or transhistorical truth.[51]

For Linda Hutcheon, the postmodern is much more an artistic style, recognizable by its self-reflexivity and irony, especially in its relations to the practices and objects of the surrounding culture and the cultural past. Postmodern work often takes the form of parody, which has a highly divided and ambivalent relation to its object of imitation. Although Hutcheon recognizes that the postmodern, as she defines it, has been commercialized and appropriated by hegemonic forces, she insists on the contestatory power, no matter how ambivalent, of postmodern art.[52]

For Jean Baudrillard and Fredric Jameson, in very different ways, postmodernism is first and foremost a social and cultural predicament. Baudrillard is interested in a history of simulacra from the Renaissance to the present, which ends in the present stage of third-order simulacra in which simulation is so widespread as to create a 'hyperreality' which has subsumed the place of nature and the real (think of Disneyland and tabloid television).[53] With the new cultural order comes a new economic and political order: 'the political economy of the sign'.[54] In light of this new proliferation of image and information, thinkers from Marx to Foucault, still concerned with production rather than reproduction, are rendered obsolescent.[55] Jameson's understanding of postmodernism is evident in the title of his book *Postmodernism, or, The Cultural Logic of Late Capitalism*.[56] For Jameson, postmodernism is the cultural predicament brought on by late capitalism's extension of commodification into virtually all aspects of social and cultural life. Cultural production under late capitalism's volatile and transient market configurations often takes the form of 'pastiche', a borrowing from anywhere without a commitment to anything, satire without any bite. The proliferation of technologies, commodities and information renders the world 'sublime', that is, complicated beyond a human scale of understanding. Only marxism, argues Jameson, can effect a 'cognitive mapping', a totalizing understanding, which would begin to make the world knowable and eventually – although not immanently – transformable.

Since Heidegger and, in a more detailed way, Marshall McLuhan, thinkers have been concerned with the effects of technology – implants, interfaces, connections, prostheses – on the human body, and the postmodern condition has only served to heighten such interests. Donna Haraway, for instance, sees the present age as enacting 'the invention and reinvention of nature – perhaps the most central arena of hope, oppression, and contestation for inhabitants of the planet earth in our times',[57] and this reinvention entails reinventing ourselves. In 'mapping the biopolitical body'[58] (whom we are made to be by social and scientific forces), Haraway sees hope in 'cyborg feminism'. Cyborgs are hybrid creatures, composed of organism and machine, and 'The cyborgs populating feminist science fiction make very problematic the statuses of man or woman, human, artefact, member of a race, individual entity, or body'.[59] Rejecting universal and totalizing theories, Haraway sees in the cyborg the possibility of transgressing and reconstructing boundaries and thereby taking responsibility for biopolitical configurations of body and self: 'The cyborg is resolutely committed to practicality, irony, intimacy, and perversity. It is oppositional, utopian, and completely without innocence.'[60]

Postmodern theory tends to combine a certain emotional distance – often an ironic or 'cool' relation to contemporary culture – with a generalized pessimism about the possibility of social change and revolution: the cultural, political and economic system that dominates the world is a truly formidable and overwhelming opponent. Even with those theorists who see promise and possibility through postmodernism (Haraway, for instance), there is a concomitant sense of danger and oppression. Often postmodern theory resembles traditional marxism in the determinist relations it draws between culture and the socio-technological order: there is no outside to the postmodern condition; all one can do is work within its possibilities and limitations. Granted, talk of revolution is often replaced with talk of transgression and subversion, but it is not completely clear what these are or what good they can do.

There are two important generalizations about postmodernism and theatre that need to be made. First, if postmodernism is the condition of contemporary culture, then all culture produced in our time is by definition postmodern. To try and single out (any more than provisionally) certain works for stylistic reasons as postmodern while ignoring others is empirically unsound and limiting. Postmodernism is as postmodernism does. One might also object that irony, allusiveness and tricks of self-referentiality are nothing new in western culture (see *The Knight of the Burning Pestle*, *Tristram Shandy* and *Ulysses*), and so what makes postmodernism so distinctive? If we begin with a narrowly stylistic definition of the postmodern, these questions remain unanswerable. All we can do is observe the particular forms and relations that postmodernism takes in any particular cultural phenomenon, although this may well result in certain patterns appearing to be 'typically' postmodern. Second, theatre *per se* is a somewhat marginal cultural activity in the postmodern world. As Baudrillard points out, theatre has gone from a dominant art form in early modern Europe to a relatively minor one in a postmodern world where everything is theatricalized, but where the theatrical is more commonly presented through television, computers, film and other technological and easily transmitted media. We have seen, in recent years, the rebirth of extravagantly spectacular musical theatre in the work of Andrew Lloyd Webber, a rebirth in a new commodified format in keeping with the markets of global capitalism; but such theatre indicates more the ability of capital to appropriate than the resurgence of theatre as a defining feature of our culture. In some thinkers and practitioners – Hélène Cixous, for instance – theatre is a residual form useful and attractive because it goes against the grain of our technological and simulated culture, promising, in a way reminiscent of phenomenological thought, an encounter with real time, lived experience and death.[61]

Some of these issues are addressed in Johannes Birringer's *Theatre, Theory, Postmodernism*.[62] Birringer laments the marginalization of theatre in postmodern culture, and while theatre's resistance to being on 'the cutting edge' is charming, it is also incapacitating.[63] Birringer does not see postmodernist late capitalism as an attractive situation – it is a time of dematerializing and dehumanizing effects on the 'dispossessed body' and of 'pervasive social and economic displacements';[64] there is no point, however, in refusing to engage with this situation. Birringer calls for theatre to have a 'critical connection to postmodern culture'.[65] Postmodernism is a process still underway and not an irresistible *fait accompli*. For Birringer, theatre's resistance to postmodern impoverishment lies not in its anachronistic 'liveness', but in its obsessive exploration of representation and its limits, in its ability to contradict and rupture the indifference of contemporary culture:

> the practices and countermodels I have described allow us to think that the theatre cannot be absorbed by the Spectacle of a technological culture as long as it can still experience and reperform the contradictions produced by this culture.[66]

A similar, even more sanguine, position is taken by Philip Auslander, who sees in performances such as the Wooster Group's *L.S.D.* and the stand up comedy of Andy Kaufman and Sandra Bernhard, instances of postmodern political resistance to the status quo of postmodern commodification. Much like Linda Hutcheon, Auslander argues that, although 'all cultural production is politically compromised', postmodern performance restores critical distance which strategically allows us to reconsider the world we live in, thereby performing a resistant political function.[67] The political critique in postmodern performance, however, is not straightforward in the way traditionally political art has been. First of all, Auslander says, the import of a work can only be seen in a subtle and complex understanding of its context.[68] Moreover, postmodern performances do not contain explicit commentary or take political positions, but raise uncertainties by representing our own compromises without taking a clear position.

Auslander's readings of both context and performance text are supple and sophisticated. There is, however, something extremely attenuated about the political resistance he claims to observe. To further understanding can be effective politics. The postmodern strategies Auslander observes, however, are often so subtle and uncertain it's not clear how much an audience is capable of appreciating them. As Auslander admits, the difference between being inside the postmodern situation and representing it is 'a small one'.[69] As an effective strategy for political resistance, it may be smaller than he thinks.

Tom Stoppard, Anna Deavere Smith and Heiner Müller

A certain kind of postmodernism – elegant if trifling – can be seen in a number of plays by Tom Stoppard, for instance *The Real Thing*. The title itself of this work indicates a postmodern concern with authenticity and simulation, which in the play is presented structurally as an opposition between real life and the stage – not exactly a stunning new analogy, but one here deployed with sophistication. The play's characters are all involved in theatre and scenes from plays in which they are acting – *'Tis Pity She's a Whore*, for instance – are interlaced abruptly with scenes of 'real life'. The play also features a pastiche and overlay of high and low cultural references: John Ford, Italian opera, the Righteous Brothers, the Crystals; this juxtaposition raises the question of the 'real thing' in art, a question left open in a typically postmodern tip of the hat to mass culture:

> I like Herman's Hermits, and the Hollies, and the Everly Brothers, and Brenda Lee, and the Supremes. . . . I don't mean everything they did. I don't like *artists*. I like singles . . . the Righteous Brothers' recording of 'You've Lost that Lovin' Feelin' on the London label [is] possibly the most haunting, the most deeply moving noise ever produced by the human spirit.[70]

An ironic scepticism is at play throughout, including in the political debate between the conservative and the proper on one hand and an impolite and awkward leftist commitment on the other. And yet there remains, along with the play of pluralism and artifice, a residing faith in art, words, love and reality which runs counter to the reputed postmodern invest-ment in overriding irony. Does this mean *The Real Thing* is not truly postmodern? Rather, we might find in it the tensions of the postmodern condition, in which tradition and the longing for certainty are bound up with a deep cultural and formal scepticism.

Anna Deavere Smith's *Twilight: Los Angeles, 1992* also exhibits many of the characteristics that have been taken to be postmodern. The play is a one-person show about the Rodney King riots in Los Angeles. Smith taped interviews with various people who experienced the riots and in performance she mimics those she interviewed, using edited transcripts of the interviews as text. Smith's procedure raises interesting questions of simulation and reality: on the one hand, she uses the exact unrehearsed words of her subjects, and spends much time perfecting their exact gestures – in this way she participates in a heightened but traditional realism. On the other hand, she learns her parts from videotape, and so technological representation lies behind her exacting verisi-militude. Moreover, as careful as she may be, her reenactments cannot escape being simulation, and distortion is inevitable – some she has interviewed have complained that she exaggerates their accents and gestures. Also, as in the theatre of Brecht, Smith does not present reality in all its wayward complexity; rather she presents character with the help of a few carefully chosen props and costumes: caps, ties, a phone, a billy club. Alice Rayner, whose work is discussed in Chapter 1, sees Smith's performance strategy, however postmodern in the detail of its situation, as 'well within the tradition' of theatre phenomenology. There is always a gap between theatre and reality, and even documentary-like representation is simulation:

> however much it uses the real in its material, [Smith's work] precludes a designation of the real and of verifiable truth. It cannot close off its representation in reference because the very acts of selecting, combining and theatricalizing dissolve the terms of the real and put them into the terms of the imaginary.[71]

Here postmodern and phenomenological analysis come together in a manner reminiscent of that of Gianni Vattimo.

Twilight: Los Angeles, 1992 is structured by fragmentation and juxtaposition: many different voices are given short monologues; no one voice is allowed the space to dominate. In this way, Smith's play escapes the master narratives discussed by Lyotard. In many ways, dramatic form, with its lack of narrative overview, is more conducive to decentred authority than many literary forms, but this effect can be heightened or diminished depending on how it is put into play – Shakespeare is more polyvocal than Shaw, for instance. Smith is interested in embracing formal and material diversity, in making a theatre which attempts to reflect the complexity of society.[72] Just as there is no one unifying voice capable of speaking for society, Smith does not present a naive solution to complex social problems. Rather, she is interested in presenting 'the *processes* of the problems'; solutions, to come later, 'will call for the participation of large and eclectic groups of people'.[73]

Twilight: Los Angeles, 1992 is rich in characters who, in the condition of sublime incomprehensibility outlined by Jameson, feel overwhelmed by forces beyond their understanding and control. Such a condition begins with the figure behind the play, Rodney King, a man at the centre of forces that reduce him to confusion and powerlessness. Most pointedly within the play itself are Walter Park and his family. Park, a Korean convenience store owner, was shot in the head during the rioting and was given a frontal lobotomy. He continues to be, at the time of the interview, heavily sedated. 'Then why, / why he has to get shot?' asks his wife, June Park, 'You know, / I don't know why.'[74]

Twilight has a number of meanings in the play. One, put forward by Homi Bhabha, whom Smith interviewed from London by phone, is that twilight is 'the moment of ambivalence / and ambiguity. / The inclarity, / the enigma, / the ambivalences'.[75] Here is another variation on the postmodern theme of confusion and incomprehensibility and the absence of master narratives. Twilight is also the name of a young black gang leader and trucemaker who is given the last speech in the play. Here Smith embraces some of the themes of postcolonialism: 'The relationships among peoples of color and *within* racial groups are getting more and more complicated,' Smith writes,[76] in a way resembling what Gayatri Spivak argues. Twilight the character embraces a perspective not unlike Edward Said's call for a hybrid identity and understanding: 'in order for me to be a, to be a true human being, / . . . I can't forever dwell in the idea, / of just identifying with people like me and understanding me and mine.'[77] In our multicultural, postmodern predicament, Smith, like Twilight, calls for 'multifaceted identities'.[78]

If there is any postmodern characteristic missing from Smith's play, it is the irony and depoliticization discussed by Hutcheon and Jameson: here is a non-ironic and committed postmodern theatre. In this way, it has been noted, Smith exhibits a politically purposeful postmodernism aligned with Habermas's belief in the possibility of complex, engaged and rational consensus and change.[79]

If the postmodern constructs a world in which human lives are, like everything else, exchangeable commodities in a shifting and inescapable market which commodifies the heretofore uncommodified and discards whatever is outmoded, then Heiner Müller and his work seem a particularly compelling example of theatre in the postmodern condition.

Müller began his career in the 1950s in what used to be called East Germany or the GDR. In the late 1970s and 1980s, he was in the rare position of working back and forth between East Germany and the west, and it was in this capacity that he became a prominent figure in international theatre. During this period, Müller often commented on the differences between society and theatre in east and west.[80] Life in the east was ultimately better: socialism gave people a sense of security and community, and the utopian drive towards a just society, although severely compromised by totalitarianism, was still alive. Because of technological and societal limitations, theatre in the east was not swamped by other media and remained a form of expression of central importance. Nonetheless, Müller was in a position to live out the 'common fantasy' of the east: 'to go to the West from time to time and to come back'.[81] Consequently, Müller's attitude to the postmodernism associated with the west was complex and contradictory. His 'Reflections on Post-Modernism' is a poetic and dense critique of the depoliticization of culture in the west.[82] In a more iconoclastic mode, Müller writes, 'The only Postmodernist I know of was August Stramm, a modernist who worked in a post office'; and yet, when asked where he would prefer to mount his plays, he answers, 'I would like to stage MACBETH on the top of the World Trade Center for an audience in helicopters'[83] – which sounds (in terms of technology, capital, the recontextualization of the past and the complicity of the artist with the established order) like a postmodern performance if ever there was one.

Many of these attitudes and tensions are played out in Müller's *Hamletmachine*, a radical adaptation of Shakespeare. Stylistically, *Hamletmachine* is typically postmodern in its fragmentation, complex irony, overlaying of cultural quotations (it ends by citing Susan Atkins of the Manson gang) and mixing of traditional and current cultural images, as in 'the madonna with breast cancer'.[84] Moreover, Müller's Hamlet finds himself in a position of privilege much like Müller's own:

> In the solitude of airports
> I breathe again I am
> A privileged person My nausea
> Is a privilege
> Protected by torture
> Barbed wire Prisons.[85]

Like Müller, Hamlet exists between a world dominated by Stalin and one dominated by Coca-Cola. As a white male, he is a spent force, but new figures of liberation arise in his place: Marx, Lenin and Mao as three naked women (Müller is interested in the rebellion of the oppressed body against what western and patriarchal power has done to it); change, when it comes, will be brought about by revolutionary, third world and feminist forces.

Hamletmachine is, however, a very bleak work, and many commentators, including Herbert Blau, have noted the despair and hopelessness in Müller's theatre – he himself has declared, 'I am neither a dope- nor a hope- dealer'.[86] Critics have been particularly troubled by Müller's collaborations with Robert Wilson – Birringer writes of Wilson's production of *Hamletmachine* 'sucking the political thought out of the images and spilling a cool, architectonic-technological brilliance over the stage'.[87] Nonetheless, Müller's bleakness in this period was tied to the possibility of a long, difficult process of social revolution.

Things have been quite different since 1989. The fall of the eastern bloc to capitalism has, first of all, erased the position from which Müller formulated his unique position: there is no longer a betwixt and between but only monolithic commodification. Much of Müller's work has become irrelevant or at least anachronistic and out of fashion. On a larger scale, East

German theatre has suffered profoundly under unification. Carl Weber notes that in the GDR 'no other medium enjoyed equal tolerance to conduct a discussion of the state's fossilized political structure', and on a strictly economic level, theatres in the GDR received large government subsidies and functioned independent of a market economy.[88] After reunification, theatres in the east have been forced to raise ticket prices drastically, thus running the risk of losing the audience that made theatre in the GDR so vital; the influx of western affluence and media further threatens the centrality of the theatre.

After reunification, Margaret Croyden finds in Müller an unmatched pessimism and a sense of tragedy and despair. Müller has even less hope than in the past:

> What I liked about the GDR was that money was not the first value and now money is the first value and this is the end of history for a while. . . .
>
> Apparently people need money and possessions, and my only hope is that one day there will be a giant nausea and a national vomiting. And then you can talk to Germans about the 'third way' [not communism, not capitalism, but something else – nobody knows what] and not before. And that will take a long time.[89]

In this spirit of *'posthistoire'*, or the end of history (for now), Müller presented in 1990 a seven-and-a-half hour *Hamlet*, including in it *Hamletmachine*, which was a 'requiem for the GDR'.[90] Andreas Höfele positions this production in a theatre of 'exhaustion' in which the possibilities of the future are exhausted and the 'potentially liveliest art has been invaded by images of stagnation, deadness, and decay'.[91] The play begins with Hamlet's dying words: 'How the play ends is a foregone conclusion; it has, in fact, ended already'; 'and in the end Fortinbras, wearing a business suit and a gold mask, a star warrior of capitalism, takes over'.[92]

3 POST-COLONIAL THEORY

Like postmodernism, post-colonialism is an attempt to describe the contemporary situation and its culture, this time by focusing on the effects of the western imperialism which has dominated the world since the sixteenth century. The term post-colonialism implies both a situation coming after colonialism and a situation in the heritage or aftermath of colonialism: both an ongoing liberation and an ongoing oppression. Like feminism, post-colonialism aims to give voice to an oppressed group by understanding and critiquing the structures of oppression and articulating and encouraging liberation and revolution. In this case the group is those who have lived under the imperialist domination of western colonial powers. In very different ways, this includes, for instance, Ireland, Canada, Australia, South Africa, Palestine, Algeria, Brazil, India and Viet Nam. Unlike much postmodern theory, post-colonial theory often combines individual emotional commitment and outrage with a defiant optimism. It is much more strident and activist than an acquiescent postmodernism.

Post-colonial theory has taken many turns, mapping the complexity of the post-colonial condition. The work of Edward Said, for instance, moves from a critique of 'orientalism', the reductive ideology and culture of western imperialism and the 'imaginative geography' which entrenches clear and asymmetrical divisions between 'orient' and 'occident' to the advantage of the west,[93] to the acknowledgement and acceptance of hybridity – the entanglement of cultural identities in a migratory and diasporic world – and the call for a subjectivity which transcends the restraints of imperial, national or provincial limits.[94] In his discussion of hybridity, Said, like many others, sees that patterns of migration have rewritten post-colonial geography as well as identity: today the post-colonial is as much a part of London, Paris, Berlin, New York and Toronto as it is of Hong Kong, Jerusalem, Soweto and Recife.

As in the thought of Walter Benjamin and much feminism, patterns of oppression for Said are to be found not only in the most egregiously jingoistic examples, but in the 'masterpieces' of the western tradition:

> Most professional humanists . . . are unable to make the connection between the prolonged and sordid cruelty of practices such as slavery, colonialist and racial oppression, and imperial subjection on the one hand, and the poetry, fiction, philosophy of the society that engages in these practices on the other.[95]

One facet of post-colonial work is to challenge the canon of western art, a challenge which takes myriad forms, from outright rejection to reappropriation and reformulation.

In *The Wretched of the Earth*, Franz Fanon writes, 'In decolonisation, there is therefore the need of a complete calling in question of the colonial situation'.[96] In post-colonial theory, this has come to mean a subtle examination of the many and often conflicting strands that make up the post-colonial situation and identity. Gayatri Chakravorty Spivak brings a powerful commitment to marxism, deconstruction (she is the translator of Derrida's *Of Grammatology*) and feminism to her analyses of the situation of the colonial 'subaltern', especially the situation of non-western women. Moreover, she is interested not only in the critique of the eurocentrism of western culture ('I teach a small number of the holders of the can(n)on, male or female, feminist or masculist, how to read their own texts, as best I can'[97]) but in understanding the complex forces that define the 'interests' of any subject position. In this light she posits not a monolithic idea of woman or brown person, but the subaltern as a divided rather than transparent subject. From marxism and especially deconstruction, Spivak takes up a call for a 'productive bafflement'[98] in which concepts, definitions and positions are always deployed provisionally and strategically and are always open to questioning and rethinking.

Homi Bhabha is concerned specifically with the discourse of colonialism, how its metaphoric and metonymic patterns structure the other as fetish and stereotype in order to reduce, dominate, discriminate against and exploit non-European peoples.[99] Imperialist ideology follows the logic of language and affect as much as it does the dictates of Enlightenment reason. For those who attempt to resist it, therefore, it is necessary to work in 'betweenness', in strategies tied to fragmentation and displacement, which can be a form of revolt against the seemingly monolithic, seemingly rational, authority of imperialism.[100] Similarly, the Vietnamese-American theorist and filmmaker Trinh T. Minh-Ha invokes the fragment which 'stands on its own and cannot be recuperated by the notion of totalizing whole'.[101] For her the post-colonial subject is constructively hybrid and unfinished and not tied to an imperialist ideal of unity and completeness. She is interested as a woman, an Asian-American and an artist in not only how 'woman, native, other' has been represented in imperialist ideology, but also, more creatively, in experimenting with the ways she can represent herself. Consequently, for example, her theoretical work, much influenced by western thinking, is interspersed with poetry and zen philosophy.[102] The east is not essentially anti-rational any more than the west is inherently rational, and any particular subject position in a world as variable as our own will call for the bringing together of disparate elements in new and unexpected ways.

Given the geographical sweep of post-colonial studies, it has proven difficult to capture a sense of the field in a single volume. Many special issues of academic journals have been dedicated to post-colonial topics; a number of readers have recently been published.[103] Bill Ashcroft, Gareth Griffiths and Helen Tiffin's *The Empire Writes Back* has provided an introduction to post-colonial theory and literatures;[104] theatre, however, has proven more elusive. Geographical disparateness is coupled with a wide range of performative practices, often paratheatrical or ritualistic, which fall outside the parameters of the western theatrical tradition. The section of *Critical Theory and Performance* dedicated to such material (which the editors have chosen to call, somewhat misleadingly, 'Cultural Studies') indicates some of the breadth that ensues: a South Indian *King Lear*; the rituals of Shamans in Thailand and Chicago; the trickster in Ntozake Shange; the Chinese American in *Yankee Dawg You Die*; political demonstrations in Tiananmen Square and Berlin, and at Kent State University; Mardi Gras in New Orleans.[105] Post-colonialism also gives rise to comparative studies of national cultures; for instance, a number of volumes have compared Canadian and Australian literature and drama, especially in terms of aboriginal work.[106]

Aimé Césaire, David Henry Hwang and Tomson Highway

In the engagement with the canon of western theatre, Ashcroft, Griffiths and Tiffin stress the importance of Shakespeare's *The Tempest* for post-colonial thought:

> *The Tempest* has been perhaps the most important text used to establish a paradigm for post-colonial readings of canonical works. So established are these readings that in contemporary productions 'some emphasis on colonialism is now expected.' In fact, more important than the simple rereading of the text itself by critics or in productions has been the widespread employment of the characters and structure of *The Tempest* as a general metaphor for imperial-marginal relations or, more widely, to characterize some specific aspect of post-colonial reality. For example, Chantal Zabus extends [George] Lamming's reading of *The Tempest* to show how writers throughout the post-colonial world, particularly writers of the Anglophone and Francophone white and Black diasporas, have written answers to *The Tempest* from the perspectives of Caliban, Miranda, and Ariel.[107]

Especially in recent backlashes against political correctness, post-colonial readings of *The Tempest* have been high profile targets of attack – Dinesh D'Souza, for instance, has called it unfair and an indignity to reduce Shakespeare to a mere function of colonial forces.[108] These attacks try to ignore the historical sources of Shakespeare's play in accounts of new world discovery and turn away from those textual moments when the colonialist implications of the relation between Caliban and others in the play are made overt and urgent. Furthermore, these attacks fail to appreciate the post-colonial reading project as it manifests itself especially in theatrical adaptation: reading is always in part political and adaptation is always a remaking with different emphases and with a new purpose.

Aimé Césaire's *A Tempest* is the foremost post-colonial adaptation of Shakespeare's play.[109] In general outline, Césaire's drama text follows Shakespeare's relatively closely, until the end when Prospero remains behind in a bitter conflict with Caliban for control of the island. Throughout, however, Césaire uses various means to change the emphasis, from Shakespeare's on romance and reconciliation to his own on imperialism, domination and struggle.

Parts of Shakespeare are retained more or less intact: fore-most is Césaire's retention of Caliban's song of freedom and defiance '*As in Shakespeare*'.[110] At other times, Césaire takes a moment from Shakespeare but expands or reformulates it: Caliban's 'You taught me your language' becomes an attack on the strategic limitations of Prospero's politico-pedagogical project:

> You didn't teach me a thing! Except to jabber in your own language so that I could understand your orders – chop the wood, wash the dishes, fish for food, plant vegetables, all because you're too lazy to do it yourself. And as for your

learning, did you ever impart any of *that* to me? No, you took care not to. All your science and know-how you keep for yourself alone, shut up in big books like those.[111]

Trinculo's discussion of putting an Indian on display in England is expanded and directed much more explicitly at Caliban.[112] In Shakespeare, Prospero tries more or less successfully to impose a chaste atmosphere on the wedding masque he stages, although thoughts of Caliban ultimately interrupt the festivities; in Césaire, Eshu, a 'black devil-god', interrupts the masque with an 'obscene' song.[113] Prospero is more completely a tyrant than he is in Shakespeare's play, and the European characters are more overtly colonizers.

In these instances, Césaire is taking his cue from something explicit or hinted at in Shakespeare. At other times, however, he adds something much less evident in the original. Most important are two new scenes, in the first of which Caliban debates with Ariel on the best way to work towards freedom, and in the second of which Caliban debates with Prospero on the nature of the imperialist project.[114] Central to Césaire's revision, Caliban has intelligence and resolve to go with his rebellion and resistance.

Césaire's *A Tempest* is labelled an 'Adaptation for a Black Theatre'. As such, it presents the events of Shakespeare's play not only from another perspective but for another audience, one for which Caliban is the hero and Prospero the monster. The play is also, however, a 'psychodrama'[115] in which black actors take up all the roles, playing out not only the external and political but also the internal and psychological structures of oppression that go with imperialist domination. Here Césaire's play begins to address the complexities of post-colonial subjectivity.

David Henry Hwang's highly successful *M. Butterfly* exhibits many of the concerns of post-colonial theory. In the tradition of Benjamin, Said and Césaire, Hwang reveals the oppressive structures at the heart of a masterpiece of western culture – this time Puccini's *Madame Butterfly*, in which Hwang sees 'a wealth of sexist and racist clichés'.[116] For Hwang, *Madame Butterfly* is a paradigm of western male attitudes toward Asia and Asian women, attitudes both profoundly mistaken and profoundly oppressive. In short, Puccini's opera is a prime example of the orientalist ideology discussed by Said. In Hwang's play, the French diplomat Gallimard, who has taken a Chinese lover, uses the music and words of the opera to help him – as in the discourse theory of Homi Bhabha – fetishize and confine his lover and their relationship. In this way Hwang explores the mind set that guides western attitudes towards the east (the play is presented as the recollections of Gallimard): in the western imaginary, the east is feminine, passive and always victimized. Both Puccini and Gallimard attempt to foist this western imaginary on eastern reality, but ultimately this vision says more about, is truer of, the west than it is the east. Hwang sees his play as 'a deconstructivist *Madame Butterfly*'[117] in which he reveals the truth behind the western cliché by turning Puccini's story upside down: in the end it is Gallimard who is the true M. Butterfly, the victim dying for unrequited love. 'I am pure imagination,' he declares. 'And in imagination I will remain.'[118]

Although he posits his play as deconstructivist, *M. Butterfly* moves inexorably towards a revelation of, literally, the naked truth. Like Césaire's Caliban, Hwang's Song Liling is a cocky and confident character who seems to have escaped all the self-destructive illusions that Gallimard brought to their relationship – indeed he has clear-headedly exploited them for twenty-five years. Hwang's play too, despite its self-reflective and theatrical toying with representation, is extremely self-assured and clear-headed. *M. Butterfly* is not interested in the more difficult areas of complicity in the post-colonial subject;

in this way Hwang's deconstruction remains strategically one-sided. Nor is there in the play – despite Hwang's own position as a Chinese-American – any interest in hybridity as a subject position. In *M. Butterfly*, east is east and west is west and never the twain shall meet.

A more complicated engagement with post-colonial subjectivity from within can be found in *Dry Lips Oughta Move to Kapuskasing*[119] by Tomson Highway, a Cree-Canadian born in northern Manitoba and now based in Toronto. *Dry Lips* is the second of seven proposed plays set on the fictional Wasaychigan Hill Indian Reserve. The first is *The Rez Sisters*, which deals with seven reserve women who travel to Toronto for the world's biggest bingo game.[120] The only male character in *The Rez Sisters* is the traditional trickster figure Nanabush. *Dry Lips*, on the other hand, features seven male characters, and Nanabush, basically a non-gendered or doubly-gendered figure, is this time female. Set side by side, the two plays reveal a symmetry in their representation of gender in native society, although it is telling that Highway has chosen in these first two plays to represent men and women on the reserve as two solitudes. Especially in *Dry Lips*, the separation echoes the tensions and power struggles between native men and women – the attempt by the reserve women to start a hockey team is taken as an affront to male control and esteem. Highway's theatre is profoundly concerned with the differences between native women and native men; at the same time, especially in the figure of Nanabush, Highway presents a place beyond simple gendered identity and oppression. Nanabush presents a native alternative to restrictive binary identities which for Highway are in large measure the imposition of western patriarchy on native culture. In a similar tension, *Dry Lips* combines a culturally acceptable, often restrictive, male homosocial structure with hints of a repressed homoeroticism which upsets the binary order from another direction.

Highway, who is gay, professes strong feminist sympathies and sees his plays in part as representations of the damage imposed by western patriarchy on native women and native communities. Nevertheless, when the play received its second production, which ran at a large, mainstream Toronto theatre, it was attacked by a number of feminist critics. Two central, horrific events in the play are the birth of a child with fetal alcohol syndrome and the rape of a young woman with a crucifix. The representation of these events in the context of an almost entirely male cast was felt by some to be inescapably misogynist. Alan Filewod has surveyed these responses and discussed the factors that went into creating such an impression: the hollowness of the large commercial theatre space; the loss of the context of the play and its relation to *The Rez Sisters*.[121] What most interests Filewod is the way responses of native women critics, uncomfortable with the production, were downplayed in the controversy. At any rate, these events reveal the complexities of post-colonialism and gender politics not only on the textual level but also on the level of reception.

Dry Lips is also complex in its relation to western culture. Ashcroft, Griffiths and Tiffin outline how the politics of language plays a major role in colonial and post-colonial projects.[122] Much of Highway's play is written in the richly textured English of the reserve; often, however, the characters speak in Cree and Ojibway, languages which, for Highway, are invested with special emotional and semantic qualities (for instance, in terms of their freedom from gender[123]). The play ends with Zachary Jeremiah Keechigeesick haltingly learning phrases in Ojibway from his wife, Hera. On a different cultural front, the play presents a conflict among the characters between Christianity and native spirituality – most localized in the differences between the tellingly named Spooky Lacroix and Simon Starblanket. Although the play's sympathies are decidedly with Nanabush and Starblanket, Highway presents the complexity of religious identity on the reserve. Finally, although Highway is outspoken in his criticisms of western patriarchy and religion, he is much more accepting of western art. Unlike *A Tempest* or *M. Butterfly*, *Dry Lips* does not take to task any masterpiece of the western canon, and Highway himself, like Edward Said, is a classical pianist, and learned much about playwriting from the English-Canadian James Reaney and the French-Canadian Michel Tremblay.

The doubleness of Highway's representation of native life can be seen in the play's tragicomic mood. On the one hand, *Dry Lips* is an extremely painful play. Its epigraph, from Lyle Longclaws, is ' . . . before the healing can take place, the poison must first be exposed . . . ' (the snake is western patriarchy, and the bitten are native males). On the other hand, it is a very funny play and, in its final moments, a joyous celebration of native beauty and life:

> The baby finally gets 'dislodged' from the blanket and emerges, naked. And the last thing we see is this beautiful naked Indian man lifting this naked baby Indian girl up in the air, his wife sitting beside them watching and laughing. Slow fade-out. Split seconds before complete black-out, Hera peals out with this magical, silvery Nanabush laugh, which is echoed and echoed by one last magical arpeggio on the harmonica, from off-stage. Finally, in the darkness, the last sound we hear is the baby's laughing voice, magnified on tape to fill the entire theater. And this, too, fades into complete silence.[124]

Augusto Boal

One area in which post-colonial thought has been particularly rich and suggestive is the theory and practice of pedagogy. Foremost in this field is the work of the Brazilian Paulo Freire, especially his seminal book, *Pedagogy of the Oppressed*.[125] Freire aligns political oppression with oppressive pedagogy.

Traditional, oppressive pedagogy is learning by rote, in which teachers who know deposit their information and ideology into the passive minds of students taken as knowing nothing on their own. Such a practice posits students – especially the oppressed – as incapable of thinking for themselves or taking up action. It also instils a sense of the unquestioned inevitability of the oppressive status quo. Against this model, Freire calls for a dialectical pedagogy in which all are thought capable of active contribution – so-called teachers can learn from so-called students. Here the oppressed bring their own experience and understanding to the pedagogical process, solving problems for themselves, and thereby training themselves to take an active role in changing the world. Freire and Henry Giroux have also developed the idea of 'border pedagogy'. Like Said's hybridity, border pedagogy takes account of patterns of migration whereby people develop a comparative sense of the relations between different environments and ways of knowing. Again like hybridity, border pedagogy calls for us to distance ourselves from our own subject positions in order to see things as others might.[126]

These pedagogical ideas have been applied to theatre in the work of Augusto Boal. The first sections of Boal's *Theatre of the Oppressed*[127] are dedicated to an elaboration of Brecht's criticisms of 'Aristotelian' theatre with the help of ideas from Freire. Aristotelian theatre, which is the hegemonic form of western theatre (Boal traces it from classical Athens down to contemporary soap operas), is a form of political indoctrination, intimidation and coercion, whereby an ideological acceptance of the status quo and fear of change is instilled in a passive and oppressed audience. For Boal, as for Brecht, the oppressive ideology and passivity of theatre are highly complicitous: the manipulative ideology of the status quo means the audience is not allowed to think for itself, and the audience's passive position as spectators means it is not allowed to act for itself.

Brecht saw this structure at work, but his epic theatre was only able to allow the audience to think and judge for itself, with its continual admonitions to the audience to find its own solutions and effects to distance them from incapacitating emotional pitfalls. Boal's project takes the next step and seeks to find ways of allowing the audience not only to think but also to act for itself, thereby turning theatre from an ideological state apparatus into 'a *rehearsal of revolution*'.[128]

Boal has proposed myriad theatre exercises in which revolutionary theatre can be enacted. A number are described in later sections of *Theatre of the Oppressed*. In an example of what he calls 'invisible theatre', actors take up places in a hotel restaurant. One of them loudly orders an elaborate meal which, it turns out, he cannot pay for. This causes a scene and the other actors start a public debate about poverty, wages, the cost of food, the right to eat and so forth. Eventually others in the restaurant, not part of the troupe, enter into the debate and the discussion goes on through the night. Here those who participate are allowed to think and speak for themselves. As Boal comments,

> In the invisible theatre the theatrical rituals are abolished; only the theatre exists, without its old, worn-out patterns. The theatrical energy is completely liberated, and the impact produced by this free theater is much more powerful and longer lasting.[129]

A second example is called '*Breaking of repression*':[130] a member of the audience relates an incident when he or she was (for reasons of race, class, sex or age) repressed, accepted the repression and acted in a manner contrary to his or her own desires. This person arranges for the actors to act out this incident. Then the scene is replayed, this time with the protagonist resisting the repression. In this way, and in discussion afterward, measure is taken of the possibilities and limitations of resistance, and the actors and audience thereby undertake a step towards revolution. For Boal, it is also important to move from the particular to the general, 'from the *phenomenon* toward the *law*'.[131] In this way Boal's poetics discourages identification with an individually fixed plight and encourages something like the hybrid and improvised thinking of the border intellectual.

Another theatrical project is called '*Knowing the Body*' and entails making the oppressed aware of the 'muscular alienation' imposed on the body by different kinds of work:

> A simple example will serve to clarify this point: compare the muscular structure of a typist with that of the nightwatchman of a factory. The first performs his or her work seated in a chair: from the waist down the body becomes, during working hours, a kind of pedestal, while the arms and fingers are active. The watchman, on the other hand, must walk continually during his eight-hour shift and consequently will develop muscular structures that facilitate walking. The bodies of both become alienated in accordance with their respective types of work.[132]

The body's shape and gestures are part of the sociopolitical 'mask' of behaviour imposed on everybody in particular ways. The task becomes to analyse and come to understand what has been done to the body in order to open up the possibility of making it and using it differently.

For Boal, traditional theatre widely conceived is 'the most perfect artistic form of coercion'.[133] Conversely, while theatre of the oppressed is not in itself a revolution, it does help prepare the way for one. In these opposed forms, Boal stresses the importance and centrality that theatre still has in our time. Such a heady emphasis might cause us to rethink the importance and meaning of theatre not only in a post-colonial context but in other contexts as well. Think, for instance, of a context most likely very present for anyone reading this book:

the theatre of the classroom. Theatre may be marginal in many activities of contemporary life, but one doesn't have to expand the idea of performance very much at all to see the classroom as a theatre and teaching and learning as a performative situation. Education may be one area in which the theatrical remains a central aspect of our culture.

What kind of performative pedagogy should we bring to the theatre classroom? Is it most important that we study the classics of the western canon or should we rather focus on the local works and performances that we undertake wherever we are: which means more to us, reading a masterpiece or mounting a small production of our own? And what forms of theatre should interest us? Should we be out in restaurants ordering meals we can't pay for, or at least undertaking something less brashly unconventional? For Boal – as for Brecht, Artaud, Blau and many others – theatre is thoughtful and, whatever form it takes, should it not make us think, especially when we undertake it in a pedagogical and intellectual context? Finally, should our study be passive or active? Should we read the classics and sit while an expert lectures to us about them, or should we get up on our feet, produce, enact and discuss? The study of theatre, as much as any discipline, brings with it the drive to make and perform rather than simply to ingest.

Many of us are highly privileged and it would depoliticize Boal's project to reduce the theatre of the oppressed by universalizing and abstracting it: if everyone is oppressed, the category loses its meaning, or at least its political import. Nonetheless, the post-colonial pedagogical and theatrical project holds exciting possibilities for situations beyond its borders narrowly drawn.

CONCLUSION: WHAT NEXT?

Every wink of an eye some new grace will be born.[1]

What is the use of talking, and there is no
      end of talking,
There is no end of things in the heart.[2]

WHAT READING?

1

If you have read this far, where does it leave you? Do you now
know theory? Some may feel they now know more than
enough: some may have begun with a dislike for theory which
has only been magnified; some may have had their initial
curiosity more than satisfied. For such readers it is time to
move on to something else. But for those whose interest in
theory has been pricked by this introduction, what is there to
do next?

There is a common academic practice in which a writer
points out the failings in all previous literature on the topic at
hand in order to argue that only his or her own new and

improved work will do. I want to end on a different tack. This book of mine has only introduced you to theory. If you want to take theory seriously, you will need many more books in order to deepen your knowledge. I want to end, therefore, not by criticizing or dismissing other works but by emphasizing their importance and the way they do things this book has not done.

Firstly, there is a vast body of work in theory which anyone undertaking the study of theory and theatre will need to attend to. The primary sources themselves, of course, are indispensable: reading *The Interpretation of Dreams*, *The Course in General Linguistics*, *Reading Capital* or *Revolution in Poetic Language* not only provides access to concepts and arguments in their fuller context but also in many cases forces an engagement with the complexity of thinking and expression which often goes hand in hand with theory. Theorizing and reading theory are not easy – as much as works such as this book attempt to make them so.

Anthologies of key selections in recent theory are the next best thing to (though ultimately no substitute for) an extensive and wide-ranging reading of theoretical works. Among others, David Lodge's *Modern Criticism and Theory: A Reader* or Dan Latimer's *Contemporary Critical Theory* provide ready access to influential and representative essays by many major theorists; a collection such as Grossberg, Nelson and Treichler's *Cultural Studies* presents more recent work, much of it varied and very current applications of important theoretical ideas.[3] More specific anthologies exist for all areas of theoretical thought from semiotics to post-colonialism and gay and lesbian and queer theory.[4] In these anthologies the reader will encounter examples of the sophisticated and individualized practice that theoretical work has increasingly become.

There are many very good introductions to theory, fuller supplements to my own work. Fredric Jameson's *The Prison House of Language*, Jonathan Culler's *Structuralist Poetics*,

Terence Hawkes' *Structuralism and Semiotics* and Terry Eagleton's *Literary Theory: An Introduction* come readily to mind.[5] These works helpfully provide a wide range of theoretical work digested by one mind and presented in one voice; often this voice speaks explicitly and bracingly from one theoretical or political position – marxist in the cases of Jameson and Eagleton. Also, there are many introductions to specific aspects of theory; for instance, the New Accents series, currently published by Routledge, includes Susan Bassnett-McGuire's *Translation Studies*, Robert C. Holub's *Reception Theory*, Christopher Norris's *Deconstruction: Theory and Practice*, and Toril Moi's *Sexual/Textual Politics*.[6] All of these introductions are useful; however, none – given the limitations of any one viewpoint and the speed with which ideas evolve in intellectual and academic production – should be taken as definitive.

In a recent, important and extremely useful consolidation, two very large encyclopedias of 'literary' theory have appeared: Irena R. Makaryk's *Encyclopedia of Contemporary Literary Theory* and Groden and Kreisworth's *Johns Hopkins Guide to Literary Theory and Criticism*.[7] These works attempt to keep up with the recent explosions in theoretical variety and have the virtues of broad coverage and a wide range of contributors' outlooks (although Makaryk's book is already behind the times in neglecting gay and lesbian and queer studies). One or both are important companions to any study of theory.

Of course, the references I provide here are meant to be merely suggestive and don't make for a complete or even adequate bibliography. Donald Marshall provides wide ranging references in his *Contemporary Critical Theory*,[8] but no bibliography in book form can hope to stay very up-to-date; various bibliographies on CD-ROM are more helpful in that regard. Such bibliographies will lead to the myriad journals of theory and theatre studies which constantly produce new work and new developments. It is in such journals that the most up-to-date theoretical work is likely to appear.

2

practical knowledge subjectival grabath

One aspect of postmodern life is the radical proliferation of *method* information. There is always more and more to read; there is *ρ* no end of things to read. Academic study in the postmodern *rehon* age partakes of the postmodern sublime: there is always too much for anyone to get his or her mind around. There is no escape from perplexity.

In such a situation, even those who wish to pursue theoretical knowledge may become overwhelmed, discouraged and intolerant. Is it necessary, one may ask oneself, to read one more essay, albeit the latest thing, on some slight yet over-trodden theoretical issue? Is the most current work always the most important work? Why? Often it seems theory is not done for the sake of fuller understanding, but because careers are riding on its continuing over-production. The result is often a kind of intellectual white noise which makes no one the wiser.

There is no end of thinking. As long as we live, we think. And there will always be unresolved issues. We will never, as hard as we try, have the answers to everything. Theory, in the sense of ongoing reflection and contemplation, is an important part of life. While theory sometimes seems overly difficult and abstruse, at other times it forces us to realize that many of life's pressing issues are complex and difficult and not susceptible to ready answers.

If we can borrow from the theatrical terminology of Peter Brook, what the reader needs to develop is the power to discern between living theory and deadly theory. Living theory can be difficult, complex and taxing; but the difficulty is necessary in order to give adequate consideration to something important. Theory, too, can be a thing in the heart. Deadly theory, on the other hand, will be verbally, notionally, gratu-itously opaque, and it will be unrelated to anything we can think of as important in our lives. Sometimes, however, it will not be easy to tell living theory and deadly theory apart, and the point is not a facile dismissal of anything we don't understand.

Finally, the postmodern age is often said to be about speed. But the most sophisticated theoretical understanding is as often about the slow contemplation of a single work or idea as it is about the rapid processing of endless volumes of information. Ignorance is not a defensible theoretical position, but each reader must decide when silence and isolation are best allowed to settle temporarily over the mind.

WHERE TO THEORY?

In the autumn of 1995 an international conference called 'Why Theatre?' was held at the University of Toronto. A major subject of discussion was the future of theatre in the twenty-first century. Given technological developments in virtual reality and communications, it is not clear what, if any, purpose will be served by live theatre in the not-too-distant future.

We could ask similar questions about the place of theory in the new century. Earlier I noted that as the old century draws to a close it is easier to see broad theoretical outlines than it might have been ten or fifteen years ago. But we still don't know what happens next. Have we come to a temporary end of theory or exhaustion of theory, analogous to the 'end of history' that has come with the global triumph of capitalism? Is it time for theory to settle down for a while? Have we seen the last of any big new movements? Perhaps, but it is just as likely that something new and unexpected is already on its way. If so, I leave you to make your own introductions.

NOTES

INTRODUCTION

1 William Shakespeare, *Hamlet*, *The Riverside Shakespeare*, ed. G. Blakemore Evans, Boston, Houghton Mifflin, 1974, 1.5.166–167.

2 Martin Heidegger, 'The Question Concerning Technology', *The Question Concerning Technology and Other Essays*, New York, Harper & Row, 1977, p. 35.

3 Ferdinand de Saussure, *Course in General Linguistics*, New York, Fontana/Collins, 1974, p. 68; Jacques Lacan, 'The Function and Field of Speech and Language in Psychoanalysis', *Écrits: A Selection*, New York, Norton, 1977, pp. 30–113; Jacques Derrida, *Of Grammatology*, Baltimore, Johns Hopkins University Press, 1976, pp. 43–44.

4 Irena R. Makaryk, ed., *Encyclopedia of Contemporary Literary Theory: Approaches, Scholars, Terms*, Toronto, University of Toronto Press, 1993; Michael Groden and Martin Kreisworth, eds, *The Johns Hopkins Guide to Literary Theory and Criticism*, Baltimore, Johns Hopkins University Press, 1994.

5 See Louky Bersianik, *The Euguélionne*, Victoria, British Columbia, Press Porcépic, n.d, and Mark Fortier, 'Cultural Studies and Theatre: From Stanislavski to the Vigil', *College Literature* 19.2, June 1992, pp. 91–97.

6 See, for example, Richard Schechner, *Performance Theory*, New York, Routledge, 1988, and Marvin Carlson, *Performance: A Critical Introduction*, London, Routledge, 1996.

7 Bonnie Maranca, 'Theatre and the University at the end of the Twentieth Century', *Performing Arts Journal* 17.2 and 17.3, May/September 1995, p. 65.

8 Catherine Belsey, *Critical Practice*, London, Routledge, 1980, p. 91.

9 Antonin Artaud, *The Theater and its Double*, New York, Grove Press, 1958, p. 69.

10 Bernard F. Dukore, *Dramatic Theory and Criticism: Greeks to Grotowski*, New York, Holt, Rinehart, 1974.

11 Marvin Carlson, *Theories of the Theatre: A Historical and Critical Survey from the Greeks to the Present*, expanded edition, Ithaca, Cornell University Press, 1993.

12 Mohammad Kowsar, 'Deleuze on Theatre: A Case Study of Carmelo Bene's *Richard III*', *Theatre Journal* 38.1, March 1986, pp. 19–33; Mohammad Kowsar, 'Lacan's *Antigone*: A Case Study in Psychoanalytic Ethics', *Critical Theory and Performance*, eds Janelle G. Reinelt and

Joseph R. Roach, Ann Arbor, University of Michigan Press, 1992, pp. 399–412; Gerald Rabkin, 'The Play of Misreading: Text/Theatre/ Deconstruction', *Performing Arts Journal* 7.1, 1983, pp. 44–60; Elinor Fuchs, 'Presence and the Revenge of Writing: Re-thinking Theatre After Derrida', *Performing Arts Journal* 9.2 and 9.3, 1985, pp. 163–173; Keir Elam, *The Semiotics of Theatre and Drama*, London, Routledge, 1980; Sue-Ellen Case, *Feminism and Theatre*, New York, Routledge, 1988; Jill Dolan, *The Feminist Spectator as Critic*, Ann Arbor, UMI Research Press, 1988; Gayle Austin, *Feminist Theories for Dramatic Research*, Ann Arbor, University of Michigan Press, 1990.

13 Two of the more recent books by Herbert Blau are *The Eye of Prey: Subversions of the Postmodern*, Bloomington, Indiana University Press, 1987, and *The Audience*, Baltimore, Johns Hopkins University Press, 1990.

14 Janelle G. Reinelt and Joseph R. Roach, *Critical Theory and Performance*, Ann Arbor, University of Michigan Press, 1992.

15 Manfred Pfister, *The Theory and Analysis of Drama*, Cambridge, Cambridge University Press, 1991.

16 Reinelt and Roach, *Critical Theory and Peformance*, pp. 1–2.

17 Herbert Blau, 'Ideology and Performance', *Theatre Journal* 35.4, December 1983, p. 459.

18 Carlson, *Theories of the Theatre*, p. 540.

19 Terry Eagleton, *Literary Theory: An Introduction*, Minneapolis, University of Minnesota Press, 1983.

CHAPTER 1: THEATRE, LIFE AND LANGUAGE

1 Ferdinand de Saussure, *Course in General Linguistics*, New York, Fontana/Collins, 1974, pp. 66–67.

2 *ibid.*, p. 68.

3 *ibid.*, pp. 20–21.

4 *ibid.*, pp. 111–112.

5 *ibid.*, p. 118.

6 *ibid.*, p. 13.

7 *ibid.*, pp. 101–102.

8 Charles Peirce, *Peirce on Signs*, ed. James Hoopes, Chapel Hill, University of North Carolina Press, 1991.

9 Roland Barthes, 'Introduction to the Structural Analysis of Narratives', *A Barthes Reader*, ed. Susan Sontag, New York, Hill & Wang, 1982, pp. 251–295.

10 Roland Barthes, *The Fashion System*, New York, Hill & Wang, 1983.

11 Roland Barthes, *Mythologies*, London, Jonathan Cape, 1972.

12 Roland Barthes, *S/Z: An Essay*, New York, Hill & Wang, 1974.

13 Roland Barthes, *A Lover's Discourse: Fragments*, New York, Hill & Wang, 1978.

14 Roland Barthes, 'The Face of Garbo', *Mythologies*, pp. 62–64; 'The Eiffel Tower', *A Barthes Reader*, pp. 236–250.

15 Roland Barthes, *The Responsibility of Forms: Critical Essays on Music, Art, and Representation*, New York, Hill & Wang, 1985.

16 Roland Barthes, *The Grain of the Voice: Interviews 1962–1980*, New York, Hill & Wang, 1985, p. 44.

17 Barthes, 'Is Painting a Language?', *The Responsibility of Forms*, pp. 149–152.

18 Barthes, 'The Grain of the Voice', *The Responsibility of Forms*, pp. 267–277.

19 Barthes, *The Grain of the Voice*, pp. 218–220.

20 Roland Barthes, 'From Work to Text', *Textual-Strategies: Perspectives in Post-Structuralist Criticism*, ed. Josué V. Harari, Ithaca, Cornell University Press, 1979, pp. 73–81.

21 Roland Barthes, 'The Death of the Author', *Modern Criticism and Theory*, ed. David Lodge, London, Longman, 1988, pp. 167–172.

22 Barthes, *The Grain of the Voice*, pp. 212–214.

23 Keir Elam, *The Semiotics of Theatre and Drama*, London, Routledge, 1980.

24 *ibid.*, p. 7.

25 Patrice Pavis, *Languages of the Stage*, New York, PAJ Publications, 1982, p. 9.

26 Patrice Pavis, 'The Interplay Between Avant-Garde Theatre and Semiology', *Performing Arts Journal* 15, 1981, pp. 75–85.

27 Marvin Carlson, *Theatre Semiotics: Signs of Life*, Bloomington, Indiana University Press, 1990, pp. xi–xviii.

28 *ibid.*, p. 121.

29 Roland Barthes, *Critical Essays*, Evanston, Illinois, Northwestern University Press, 1972, pp. 71, 74.

30 Bertolt Brecht, *Brecht on Theatre: The Development of an Aesthetic*, New York, Hill & Wang, 1964, pp. 24, 26, 14, 31.

31 Barthes, *Critical Essays*, p. 34.

32 *ibid.*, p. 41.

33 *ibid.*, pp. 41–50.

34 Brecht, *On Theatre*, pp. 121–129.

35 *ibid.*, p. 194.

36 Quoted in Marvin Carlson, *Theories of the Theatre: A Historical and Critical Survey from the Greeks to the Present*, expanded edition, Ithaca, Cornell University Press, 1993, p. 499.

37 Brecht, *On Theatre*, pp. 204, 277.

38 Barthes, *Critical Essays*, pp. 38, 74.

39 *ibid.*, p. 49.

40 Barthes, *The Responsibility of Forms*, p. 92.

41 Walter Benjamin, *The Origin of German Tragic Drama*, London, NLB, 1977.

42 *ibid.*, pp. 175, 177.

43 *ibid.*, pp. 193, 186.

44 *ibid.*, pp. 217–218.

45 Barthes, *Critical Essays*, pp. 72–73.

46 Patrice Pavis, 'Problems of Translation for the Stage: Interculturalism and Post-modern Theatre', *The Play Out of Context: Transferring Plays from Culture to Culture*, eds Hanna Scolnikov and Peter Holland, Cambridge, Cambridge University Press, 1987, p. 41.

47 Quoted in Carlson, *Theories of the Theatre*, p. 518.

48 Michel Foucault, 'Theatrum Philosophicum', *Language, Counter-Memory, Practice: Selected Essays and Interviews*, Ithaca, Cornell University Press, 1977, p. 168.

49 Quoted in Pavis, 'The Interplay Between Avant-Garde Theatre and Semiology', p. 84.

50 Heiner Müller, 'The Walls of History', *Semiotext(e)* 4.2, 1982, p. 65.

51 Edmund Husserl, *The Idea of Phenomenology*, The Hague, Martinus Nijhoff, 1964; Martin Heidegger, *Basic Writings*, New York, Harper & Row, 1977; Jean-Paul Sartre, *Being and Nothingness: An Essay on Phenomenological Ontology*, New York, Washington Square Press, 1966; Gaston Bachelard, *The Poetics of Space*, New York, Orion Press, 1964.

52 Maurice Merleau-Ponty, *Phenomenology of Perception*, London, Routledge, 1962.

53 Martin Heidegger, 'The Question Concerning Technology', *The Question Concerning Technology and Other Essays*, New York, Harper & Row, 1977, pp. 3–35.

54 Martin Heidegger, 'The Origin of the Work of Art', *Poetry, Language, and Truth*, New York, Harper & Row, 1975.

55 Terry Eagleton, *Literary Theory: An Introduction*, Minneapolis, University of Minnesota Press, 1983, pp. 54–66.

56 Judith Butler, 'Performative Acts and Gender Constitution: An Essay in Phenomenology and Feminist Theory', *Performing Feminisms: Feminist Critical Theory and Theatre*, ed. Sue-Ellen Case, Baltimore, Johns Hopkins University Press, 1990, pp. 270–282.

57 Gianni Vattimo, *The End of Modernity: Nihilism and Hermeneutics in Postmodern Culture*, Baltimore, Johns Hopkins University Press, 1988.

58 Bert O. States, *Great Reckonings in Little Rooms: On the Phenomenology of Theater*, Berkeley, University of California Press, 1985.

59 Spalding Gray, *Monster in a Box*, New York, Vintage, 1992, pp. 69–70.

60 Bert O. States, 'The Phenomenological Attitude', *Critical Theory and Performance*, eds Janelle G. Reinelt and Joseph R. Roach, Ann Arbor, University of Michigan Press, 1992, p. 378.

61 Alice Rayner, *To Act, To Do, To Perform: Drama and the Phenomenology of Action*, Ann Arbor, University of Michigan Press, 1994, p. 4.

62 *ibid.*, p. 10.

63 See Carlson, *Theories of the Theatre*, pp. 295–296.

64 See Gregory Battcock and Robert Nickas, eds, *The Art of Performance: A Critical Anthology*, New York, Dutton, 1984, p. 326.

65 Constantin Stanislavski, *My Life in Art*, New York, Theatre Arts Books, 1948.

66 *ibid.*, p. 483.

67 *ibid.*, pp. 464–466.

68 *ibid.*, p. 462.

69 *ibid.*, pp. 483, 332.

70 *ibid.*, p. 334.

71 *ibid.*, pp. 535, 570.

72 *ibid.*, p. 566.

73 *ibid.*, p. 327.

74 *ibid.*, pp. 571–572.

75 Zbigniew Osinski, *Grotowski and his Laboratory*, New York, PAJ Publications, 1986, pp. 27–30.

76 Anton Chekhov, *Five Major Plays*, New York, Bantam, 1982, p. 74.

77 *ibid.*, pp. 92–93.

78 *ibid.*, pp. 97, 100.

79 *ibid.*, pp. 161, 154.

80 *ibid.*, p. 149.

81 *ibid.*, pp. 133, 187.

82 *ibid.*, pp. 173, 180.

83 *ibid.*, p. 92.

84 *ibid.*, p. 180.

85 *ibid.*, p. 118.
86 *ibid.*, p. 187.
87 *ibid.*, pp. 180, 143.
88 *ibid.*, p. 79.
89 *ibid.*, p. 76.
90 Stanislavski, *My Life*, p. 355.
91 Chekhov, *Plays*, p. 82.
92 *ibid.*, p. 114.
93 Jacques Derrida, 'Structure, Sign and Play in the Discourse of the Human Sciences', *Writing and Difference*, Chicago, University of Chicago Press, 1978, pp. 278–293.
94 Jacques Derrida, *Of Grammatology*, Baltimore, Johns Hopkins University Press, 1976.
95 Jacques Derrida, 'But Beyond . . . (Open Letter To Anne McClintock and Rob Nixon)', *Critical Inquiry* 13.1, Autumn 1986, p. 165.
96 Jacques Derrida, 'An Interview with Jacques Derrida', James Kearns and Ken Newton, *The Literary Review* 14, April 18–May 1, 1980, p. 22.
97 Jacques Derrida, 'Signature Event Context', *Limited Inc*, Evanston, Illinois, Northwestern University Press, 1988, pp. 1–23.
98 Jacques Derrida, *The Ear of the Other: Otobiography, Transference, Translation*, New York, Schocken, 1985.
99 Jacques Derrida, '"Eating Well", or the Calculation of the Subject: An Interview with Jacques Derrida', *Who Comes After the Subject?*, eds Eduardo Cadava, Peter Connor and Jean-Luc Nancy, New York, Routledge, 1991, p. 108.
100 Jacques Derrida, 'The Law of Genre', *Glyph* 7, Spring 1980, pp. 202–232.
101 Paul de Man, *The Rhetoric of Romanticism*, New York, Columbia University Press, 1984.
102 Paul de Man, *The Resistance to Theory*, Minneapolis, University of Minnesota Press, 1986.
103 Paul de Man, *Allegories of Reading: Figural Language in Rousseau, Nietzsche, Rilke, and Proust*, New Haven, Yale University Press, 1979.
104 Jürgen Habermas, *Communication and the Evolution of Society*, London, Heinemann, 1979.
105 Gerald Rabkin, 'The Play of Misreading: Text/Theatre/Deconstruction', *Performing Arts Journal* 19, 1983, p. 51.
106 Elinor Fuchs, 'Presence and the Revenge of Writing: Re-thinking Theatre After Derrida', *Performing Arts Journal* 26/27, 1985, p. 172.
107 *ibid.*, p. 165.

108 Stratos E. Constantinidas, *Theatre under Deconstruction: A Question of Approach*, New York, Garland, 1993, p. 291.

109 Derrida, *Of Grammatology*, p. 8.

110 Derrida, *Writing and Difference*, pp. 169–195, 232–250.

111 Antonin Artaud, *Theater and its Double*, New York, Grove Press, 1958, p. 7.

112 Antonin Artaud, *Selected Writings*, Berkeley, University of California Press, 1988, p. 160.

113 Artaud, *The Theater and its Double*, p. 13.

114 Artaud, *Selected Writings*, p. 110.

115 Artaud, *The Theater and its Double*, p. 31.

116 Artaud, *Selected Writings*, p. 155.

117 Artaud, *The Theater and its Double*, pp. 116, 146.

118 *ibid.*, p. 24.

119 Derrida, *Writing and Difference*, p. 327.

120 *ibid.*, p. 183.

121 Artaud, *Selected Writings*, pp. 83–85.

122 Derrida, *Writing and Difference*, p. 235.

123 *ibid.*, p. 194.

124 *ibid.*, p. 234.

125 *ibid.*, p. 248.

126 Artaud, *Selected Writings*, p. 155.

127 Artaud, *The Theater and its Double*, p. 146.

128 Artaud, *Selected Writings*, p. 577.

129 Artaud, *The Theater and its Double*, p. 51.

130 Artaud, *Selected Writings*, p. 86.

131 Derrida, *Writing and Difference*, p. 325.

132 Jerzy Grotowski, *Towards a Poor Theatre*, London, Methuen, 1975, p. 85.

133 *ibid.*, p. 93.

134 *ibid.*, p. 86.

135 Northrop Frye, *Words with Power: Being a Second Study of 'The Bible and Literature'*, San Diego, Harcourt Brace, 1990, p. 69.

136 Herbert Blau, *Blooded Thought: Occasions of Theatre*, New York, Performing Arts Journal Publications, 1982, p. xiii; 'Elsinore: An Analytic Scenario', *Cream City Review* 6.2, 1981, p. 83; *The Eye of Prey: Subversions of the Postmodern*, Bloomington, Indiana University Press, 1987, p. xvii.

137 Herbert Blau, *Crooked Eclipses: A Theatrical Essay on Shakespeare's Sonnets*, unpublished play, n.d.

138 Herbert Blau, 'Ideology and Performance', *Theatre Journal* 35.4, December 1983, p. 460.

139 Blau, *Eye of Prey*, p. 164; *Take Up the Bodies: Theater at the Vanishing Point*, Urbana, University of Illinois Press, 1982, p. 262; *Eye of Prey*, p. 243.

140 Blau, *Elsinore*, p. 61.

141 Blau, 'Ideology and Performance', p. 457.

142 Blau, *Take Up the Bodies*, p. 169.

143 Blau, *Crooked Eclipses*, p. 26.

144 Herbert Blau, 'The Audition of Dream and Events', *Drama Review* 31.3, Fall 1987, pp. 68, 70.

145 Blau, *Take Up the Bodies*, p. 31; *Eye of Prey*, p. 205.

CHAPTER 2: SUBJECTIVITY AND THEATRE

1 The Performance Group, *Dionysus in 69*, ed. Richard Schechner, New York, Farrar, Strauss & Giroux, 1970, n.p.

2 Two important works for understanding subjectivity and agency are Louis Althusser, 'Ideology and Ideological State Apparatuses (Notes towards an investigation)', *Lenin and Philosophy and Other Essays*, London, NLB, 1971, pp. 123–173, and Paul Smith, *Discerning the Subject*, Minneapolis, University of Minnesota Press, 1988.

3 Sigmund Freud, *The Standard Edition of the Complete Psychological Works*, ed. James Strachey, 23 vols, London, Hogarth Press, 1953–1966.

4 Freud, *Standard Edition*, vol. 18, pp. 14–15.

5 Jacques Lacan, *Écrits: A Selection*, New York, Norton, 1977.

6 Jacques Lacan, 'Of Structure as an Inmixing of an Otherness Prerequisite to Any Subject Whatever', *The Languages of Criticism and the Sciences of Man: The Structuralist Controversy*, eds Richard Macksey and Eugenio Donato, Baltimore, Johns Hopkins University Press, 1970, p. 188.

7 Jacques Lacan and the *école freudienne*, *Feminine Sexuality*, eds Juliet Mitchell and Jacqueline Rose, New York, Norton, 1982.

8 Julia Kristeva, *Revolution in Poetic Language*, New York, Columbia University Press, 1984.

9 Gilles Deleuze and Félix Guattari, *Anti-Oedipus*, New York, Viking, 1977; *A Thousand Plateaus: Capitalism and Schizophrenia*, Minneapolis, University of Minnesota Press, 1987.

10 Deleuze and Guattari, *A Thousand Plateaus*, pp. 12–13.

11 Gilles Deleuze and Félix Guattari, *Kafka: Toward a Minor Literature*, Minneapolis, University of Minnesota Press, 1986.

12 See, for example, references throughout *The Interpretation of Dreams*, *Standard Edition*, vols 4 and 5.

13 Lacan's reading of *Antigone* is discussed by Mohammad Kowsar in 'Lacan's *Antigone*: A Case Study in Psychoanalytical Ethics', *Critical Theory and Performance*, eds Janelle G. Reinelt and Joseph R. Roach, Ann Arbor, University of Michigan Press, 1992, pp. 399–412; Jacques Lacan, 'Desire and the Interpretation of Desire in *Hamlet*', *Yale French Studies* 55/56, 1977, pp. 11–52.

14 Sigmund Freud, 'Leonardo da Vinci and a Memory of his Childhood', *Standard Edition*, vol. 9, pp. 59–138.

15 Jacques Lacan, 'Seminar on "The Purloined Letter"', *Yale French Studies* 48, 1972, pp. 39–72.

16 Fred C. Alford, *The Psychoanalytic Theory of Greek Tragedy*, New Haven, Yale University Press, 1992; Walter A. Davis, *Get the Guests: Psychoanalysis, Modern American Drama, and the Audience*, Madison, University of Wisconsin Press, 1994.

17 Robert J. Landy, *Persona and Performance: The Meaning of Role in Drama, Therapy, and Everyday Life*, London, Jessica Kingsley Publishers, 1993, p. 7.

18 Spalding Gray, *Impossible Vacation*, New York, Knopf, 1992.

19 Spalding Gray, *Monster in a Box*, New York, Vintage, 1992.

20 *ibid.*, p. 16.

21 *ibid.*, p. 64.

22 *ibid.*, pp. 45–46.

23 Herbert Blau, 'Ideology and Performance', *Theatre Journal* 35.4, December 1983, p. 441.

24 Gilles Deleuze, 'Un Manifeste de Moins', *Superpositions*, Carmelo Bene and Gilles Deleuze, Paris, Editions de Minuit, 1979.

25 Slavoj Žižek, *Looking Awry: An Introduction to Jacques Lacan through Popular Culture*, Cambridge, Mass., MIT Press, 1991, pp. 9–12.

26 Slavoj Žižek, *Enjoy Your Symptom!: Jacques Lacan in Hollywood and Out*, New York, Routledge, 1992, p. 25n.18.

27 Slavoj Žižek, *The Sublime Object of Ideology*, London, Verso, 1989, p. 230.

28 *ibid.*, p. 212.

29 *ibid.*, p. 5.

30 Žižek, *Looking Awry*, p. 68.

31 Žižek, *Enoy Your Symptom!*, pp. 174–179.

32 Hélène Cixous, *Portrait of Dora, Benmussa Directs: Portrait of Dora and the Singular Life of Albert Nobbs*, London, John Calder, 1976; *The Name of Oedipus: Song of the Forbidden Body, Plays by French and Francophone Women: A Critical Anthology*, eds Christiane P. Makward and Judith G. Miller, Ann Arbor, University of Michigan Press, 1994, pp. 247–326.

33 Sue-Ellen Case, *Feminism and Theatre*, New York, Routledge, 1988; Jill Dolan, *The Feminist Spectator as Critic*, Ann Arbor, UMI Research Press, 1988; Gayle Austin, *Feminist Theories for Dramatic Research*, Ann Arbor, University of Michigan Press, 1990.

34 Elaine Aston, *An Introduction to Feminism and Theatre*, London, Routledge, 1995.

35 Austin, *Feminism and Theatre*, p. 27.

36 See, for instance, Reinelt and Roach, *Critical Theory and Performance*, p. 226.

37 Virginia Woolf, *A Room of One's Own*, London, Grafton, 1977, pp. 46–47.

38 Ann-Marie MacDonald, *Goodnight Desdemona (Good Morning Juliet)*, Toronto, Coach House Press, 1990.

39 bell hooks, 'bell hooks Speaking about Paulo Freire – The Man, His Work', *Paulo Freire: A Critical Encounter*, eds Peter McLaren and Peter Leonard, London, Routledge, 1993, p.148.

40 Laura Mulvey, 'Visual Pleasure and Narrative Cinema', *Screen* 16.3, Autumn 1975, pp. 6–18.

41 See, for example, the discussion of the work of the nineteenth-century Canadian playwright Sarah-Anne Curzon in Heather Jones, 'Feminism and Nationalism in Domestic Melodrama: Gender, Genre, and Canadian Identity', *Essays in Theatre* 8.1, November 1989, pp. 5–14.

42 Anne Russell, ed., 'Introduction', Aphra Behn, *The Rover or The Banished Cavaliers*, Peterborough, Ontario, Broadview Press, 1994, p. 31.

43 Susan Carlson, 'Cannibalizing and Carnivalizing: Reviving Aphra Behn's *The Rover*', *Theatre Journal* 47.4, December 1995, pp. 522, 539.

44 Hélène Cixous, 'Sorties: Out and Out: Attacks/Ways Out/Forays', *The Newly Born Woman*, Hélène Cixous and Catherine Clément, Minneapolis, University of Minnesota Press, 1986, pp. 63–132.

45 Case, *Feminism and Theatre*, p. 95.

46 See, for example, bell hooks, 'Representing Whiteness in the Black Imagination', and Michelle Wallace, 'Negative Images: Towards a Black Feminist Cultural Criticism', *Cultural Studies*, eds Lawrence

Grossberg, Cary Nelson and Paula Treichler, New York, Routledge, 1992, pp. 338–346, 654–671.

47 Barbra Christian, 'The Race for Theory', *Feminist Studies* 14, Spring 1988, pp. 67–79.

48 Teresa de Lauretis, 'Sexual Indifference and Lesbian Representation', Sue-Ellen Case, ed., *Performing Feminisms: Feminist Critical Theory and Theatre*, Baltimore, Johns Hopkins University Press, 1990, p. 21.

49 Jill Dolan, 'Practicing Cultural Disruptions: Gay and Lesbian Representation and Sexuality', *Critical Theory and Performance*, pp. 270, 273n.17, 272.

50 *ibid.*, p. 270.

51 Caryl Churchill, *Cloud Nine, Plays: One*, London, Methuen, 1985, pp. 251, 258.

52 *ibid.*, p. 251.

53 *ibid.*, p. 246.

54 *ibid.*, p. 307.

55 *ibid.*, p. 303.

56 *ibid.*, p. 246.

57 *ibid.*, p. 319.

58 *ibid.*, p. 308.

59 Marc Silverstein, '"Make Us The Women We Can't Be:" Cloud Nine and The Female Imaginary', *Journal of Dramatic Theory and Criticism* 8.2, Spring 1994, p. 20.

60 Ntozake Shange, *for colored girls who have considered suicide / when the rainbow is enuf, Plays: One*, London, Methuen, 1992, pp. 3–64.

61 *ibid.*, p. xvii.

62 *ibid.*, p. 4.

63 *ibid.*, p. 27.

64 *ibid.*, p. 63.

65 Barbara Lewis, 'Back Over the Rainbow', *American Theatre* 12.7, September 1995, p. 6.

66 Catherine Wiley, review of *for colored girls who have considered suicide/ when the rainbow is enuf, Theatre Journal* 43, 1991, pp. 381–382.

67 Eve Kosofsky Sedgwick, *The Epistemology of the Closet*, Berkeley, University of California Press, 1990, p. 1.

68 Adrienne Rich, 'Compulsory Heterosexuality and Lesbian Experience', *Signs* 5, Summer 1980, pp. 631–660.

69 Michel Foucault, *Power/Knowledge: Selected Interviews and Other Writings 1972–1977*, New York, Pantheon, 1980, p. 191; Julia Kristeva, 'Women's Time', *Signs* 7.1, 1981, p. 35.

70 Charles McNulty, 'The Queer as Drama Critic', *Theater* 24.2, 1993, p. 12.

71 See, for example, Donald Morton, 'Birth of the Cyberqueer', *PMLA* 110.3, May 1995, pp. 369–381.

72 Jonathan Goldberg, ed., *Queering the Renaissance*, Durham, North Carolina, Duke University Press, 1994.

73 Marjorie Garber, *Vested Interests: Cross Dressing and Cultural Anxiety*, New York, Routledge, 1992.

74 Katie Laris, review of *As You Like It*, *Theatre Journal* 47.2, May 1995, p. 301.

75 Robert Wallace, 'Towards a Poetics of Gay Male Theatre', *Essays on Canadian Writing* 54, Winter 1994, pp. 212–236.

76 Tony Kushner, *Angels in America, Part One: Millennium Approaches*, New York, Theatre Communications Group, 1993; *Angels in America, Part Two: Perestroika*, New York, Theatre Communications Group, 1994.

77 Kushner, *Perestroika*, p. 148.

78 David Savran, 'The Theatre of the Fabulous: An Interview With Tony Kushner', Per Brask, ed., *Essays on Kushner's Angels*, Winnipeg, Blizzard Publishing, 1995, p. 138.

79 *ibid.*, p. 132.

80 Kushner, *Millenium Approaches*, pp. 45–46.

81 Kushner, *Perestroika*, p. 48.

82 *ibid.*, p. 8.

83 Savran, 'Theatre of the Fabulous', p. 144.

84 David Savran, 'Ambivalence, Utopia, and a Queer Sort of Materialism: How *Angels in America* Reconstructs the Nation', *Theatre Journal* 47.2, May 1995, p. 208.

85 Wolfgang Iser, *The Act of Reading: A Theory of Aesthetic Response*, Baltimore, Johns Hopkins University Press, 1978.

86 Hans Robert Jauss, *Toward an Aesthetic of Reception*, Minneapolis, University of Minnesota Press, 1982.

87 Roland Barthes, *S/Z*, New York, Hill & Wang, 1974, p. 4.

88 Stanley Fish, *Is There a Text in This Class? The Authority of Interpretive Communities*, Cambridge, Mass., Harvard University Press, 1980.

89 Tony Bennett, *Formalism and Marxism*, London, Methuen, 1977, pp. 167–168, 137.

90 Terry Eagleton, *Walter Benjamin or Towards a Revolutionary Criticism*, London, Verso, 1981, p. 113.

91 Theo Hermans, ed., *The Manipulation of Literature: Studies in Literary Translation*, London, Croom Helm, 1983.

92 Jacques Derrida, 'Des Tours de Babel', *Difference in Translation*, ed. Joseph F. Graham, Ithaca, Cornell University Press, 1985, pp. 165–207.

93 Jacques Derrida, *The Ear of the Other: Otobiography, Transference, Translation*, New York, Schocken, 1985, pp. 157–158.

94 Paul de Man, *Allegories of Reading*, New Haven, Yale University Press, 1979.

95 Marvin Carlson, *Theatre Semiotics: Signs of Life*, Bloomington, Indiana University Press, 1990, p. 99.

96 *ibid.*, p. 113.

97 Susan Bennett, *Theatre Audiences: A Theory of Production and Reception*, London, Routledge, 1990.

98 Gerald Rabkin, 'Is There a Text On This Stage: Theatre/Authorship/ Interpretation', *Performing Arts Journal* 26/27, 1985, pp. 158, 157.

99 David Mamet, *Oleanna*, New York, Pantheon, 1992.

100 Louis MacPherson, '*Oleanna* Highlights Political Correctness as Next Big Threat', University of Toronto *Varsity*, 20 October, 1994, p. 5.

101 Bronwyn Drainie, 'Oleanna's Popularity is Deeply Disturbing', Toronto *Globe and Mail*, November 17, 1994, p. E5.

102 Kerr Huffman, '*Oleanna* and *Disclosure* Attack Sexual Harassment in the Work Place', University of Toronto *Varsity*, 8 December, 1994, p. 15.

103 For an overview of the controversy surrounding the play, see Daniel Mufson, 'Sexual Perversity in Viragos', *Theater* 24.1, 1993, pp. 111–113. Mufson ultimately fixes the play as one-sided and sexist.

104 Peter Brook, *The Shifting Point*, New York, Harper & Row, 1987, p. 87; Ralph Berry, *On Directing Shakespeare: Interviews with Contemporary Directors*, London, Croom Helm, 1977, p. 128.

105 David Selbourne, *The Making of A MIDSUMMER NIGHT'S DREAM: An Eye-witness Account of Peter Brook's Production from First Rehearsal to Opening Night*, London, Methuen, 1982, pp. 19, 65.

106 *ibid.*, pp. 79, 93, 137, 181, 219, 229, 67.

107 *ibid.*, pp. 13, 17, 21, 41, 65.

108 Berry, *On Directing Shakespeare*, p. 124.

109 Peter Brook, *The Empty Space*, New York, Atheneum, 1968, pp. 10, 12.

110 Brook, *Shifting Point*, p. 71; Berry, *On Directing Shakespeare*, p. 123.

111 Brook, *Shifting Point*, p. 45.

112 *ibid.*, pp. 71, 45, 125, 9.

113 *ibid.*, pp. 45, 9.

114 Berry, *On Directing Shakespeare*, p. 115.

115 *ibid.*, p. 130.

116 Brook, *Shifting Point*, pp. 16, 55.

117 Quoted in Glenn Loney, ed., *Peter Brook's Production of Shakespeare's* A Midsummer Night's Dream *for the Royal Shakespeare Company: The Complete and Authorized Acting Edition*, Stratford, Royal Shakespeare Company, 1974, p. 13.

118 Selbourne, *Making*, pp. 39, 217; Loney, *Acting Edition*, p. 25.

119 Berry, *On Directing Shakespeare*, p. 121; Brook, *Empty Space*, p. 12.

120 Selbourne, *Making*, pp. 101, 99.

121 *ibid.*, p. 37; Brook, *Empty Space*, p. 13.

122 Loney, *Acting Edition*, p. 54.

123 Brook, *Empty Space*, pp. 13, 16.

124 Selbourne, *Making*, pp. 29, 83, 85, 109, 139, 175, 297, 323.

125 Berry, *On Directing Shakespeare*, p. 125; Loney, *Acting Edition*, pp. 72, 70, 17, 56.

126 Loney, *Acting Edition*, p. 3a.

127 Brook, *Empty Space*, p. 14.

128 Selbourne, *Making*, pp. 279, 273.

129 *ibid.*, p. 77.

130 Loney, *Acting Edition*, pp. 28, 58.

131 *ibid.*, p. 57; Brook, *Empty Space*, p. 15.

132 Selbourne, *Making*, p. xxvi.

133 *ibid.*, pp. 293, 327, 311; Loney, *Acting Edition*, p. 35.

134 Loney, *Acting Edition*, p. 46a.

135 Selbourne, *Making*, p. xxvii.

136 Kenneth McClellan, *Whatever Happened to Shakespeare?*, London, Vision, 1978, pp. 9–10.

137 Selbourne, *Making*, p. 7.

138 *ibid.*, pp. 215, 267, 319, 321, 167.

139 Brook, *Empty Space*, pp. 127–128.

140 Selbourne, *Making*, pp. 299, 207–213, 285; Loney, *Acting Edition*, p. 76.

CHAPTER 3: WORLD AND THEATRE

1 Andrew Gurr, *Playgoing in Shakespeare's London*, Cambridge, 1987, p. 3.

2 Edward Bond, 'To the Audience', *Lear*, London, Methuen, 1983, pp. xliv–xiv.

3 Karl Marx, *Capital*, vol. 1, New York, Vintage, 1977, p. 875.

4 N. N. Feltes, *Modes of Production of Victorian Novels*, Chicago, University of Chicago Press, 1986.

5 Louis Althusser, 'Ideology and Ideological State Apparatuses (Notes towards an Investigation)', *Lenin and Philosophy and Other Essays*, London, NLB, 1971, pp. 123–173.

6 Pierre Macherey, *A Theory of Literary Production*, London, Routledge, 1978.

7 Raymond Williams, *Marxism and Literature*, Oxford, Oxford University Press, 1977, pp. 121–127.

8 Fredric Jameson, *The Political Unconscious: Narrative as a Socially Symbolic Act*, Ithaca, Cornell University Press, 1981, pp. 32–38.

9 Theodor Adorno, *Aesthetic Theory*, London, Routledge, 1984.

10 Louis Althusser, *For Marx*, London, Verso, 1969, p. 113.

11 See, for instance, Chantal Mouffe, 'Radical Democracy: Modern or Postmodern?' and Ernesto Laclau, 'Politics and the Limits of Modernity', both in *Universal Abandon? The Politics of Postmodernism*, ed. Andrew Ross, Minneapolis, University of Minnesota Press, 1988.

12 Jonathan Dollimore and Alan Sinfield, eds, *Political Shakespeare: New Essays in Cultural Materialism*, Ithaca, Cornell University Press, 1985.

13 Terry Eagleton, *Ideology: An Introduction*, London, Verso, 1991.

14 Walter Benjamin, 'N [RE THE THEORY OF KNOWLEDGE, THEORY OF PROGRESS]', *Benjamin: Philosophy, History, Aesthetics*, ed. Gary Smith, Chicago, University of Chicago Press, 1989, p. 50.

15 Walter Benjamin, 'Theses on the Philosophy of History', *Illuminations*, New York, Schocken, 1969, p. 256.

16 Michel Foucault, *The History of Sexuality*, vol. 1, New York, Vintage, 1980.

17 Michel Foucault, *Power/Knowledge: Selected Interviews and Other Writings 1972–1977*, New York, Pantheon, 1980, p. 208.

18 Michel Foucault, *The Order of Things: An Archeology of the Human Sciences*, New York, Vintage, 1973, p. 387.

19 Walter Cohen, *Drama of a Nation: Public Theater in Renaissance England and Spain*, Ithaca, Cornell University Press, 1985, pp. 189–190.

20 Robert Wallace, *Producing Marginality: Theatre and Criticism in Canada*, Saskatoon, Fifth House, 1990, pp. 97–105.

21 Richard Paul Knowles, 'From Nationalist to Multinational: The Stratford Festival, Free Trade, and the Discourses of Intercultural Tourism', unpublished paper, 1994, p. 2.

22 Richard Paul Knowles, 'Shakespeare, 1993, and the Discourses of the Stratford Festival, Ontario', *Shakespeare Quarterly* 42.2, Summer 1994, p. 225.

23 Jonathan Dollimore, *Radical Tragedy: Religion, Ideology and Power in the Drama of Shakespeare and his Contemporaries*, Chicago, University of Chicago Press, 1984, p. 4.

24 *ibid.*, p. 5.

25 *ibid.*, p. 198.

26 See, for example, Stephen Greenblatt, *Shakespearean Negotiations: The Circulation of Social Energy in Renaissance England*, Berkeley, University of California Press, 1988.

27 Bertolt Brecht, 'Study of the First Scene of Shakespeare's '*Coriolanus*', *Brecht on Theatre*, New York, Hill & Wang, 1964, pp. 259, 265.

28 *ibid.*, p. 255.

29 *ibid.*, p. 256.

30 *ibid.*, p. 254.

31 *ibid.*, pp. 252, 264.

32 *ibid.*, pp. 255, 265.

33 *ibid.*, pp. 257–258.

34 *ibid.*, pp. 262–263.

35 *ibid.*, p. 255.

36 *ibid.*, p. 259.

37 Michel Foucault, 'Of Other Spaces', *Diacritics* 16.1, Spring 1986, pp. 24–27.

38 Forest Pyle, *The Ideology of Imagination: Subject and Society in the Discourse of Romanticism*, Stanford, Stanford University Press, 1995, pp. 173–175.

39 Jameson, *The Political Unconscious*, pp. 281–299.

40 Cohen, *Drama of a Nation*, p. 391.

41 Paulo Freire, *Pedagogy of Hope: Reliving Pedagogy of the Oppressed*, New York, Continuum, 1994, p. 8.

42 Raymond Williams, *Towards 2000*, London, Chatto & Windus, 1983, p. 240.

43 Northrop Frye, 'Introduction', William Shakespeare, *The Tempest, The Complete Works*, ed. Alfred Harbage, London, Penguin, 1969, p. 1371.

44 Northrop Frye, *Northrop Frye on Shakspeare*, Markham, Ontario, Fitzhenry & Whiteside, 1986, p. 184.

45 For an overview of this history, see Ioan Davies, *Cultural Studies and Beyond: Fragments of Empire*, London, Routledge, 1995.

46 For a fuller discussion of these issues, see Lawrence Grossberg, Cary Nelson and Paula Treichler, eds, 'Cultural Studies: An Introduction', *Cultural Studies*, New York, Routledge, 1992, pp. 1–16.

47 Antony Easthope and Kate McGowan, *A Critical and Cultural Theory Reader*, Toronto, University of Toronto Press, 1993.

48 Gary Taylor, *Reinventing Shakespeare: A Cultural History from the Restoration to the Present*, New York, Weidenfeld & Nicolson, 1989, p. 6; Graham Holderness, ed., *The Shakespeare Myth*, Manchester, Manchester University Press, 1988, p. xvi.

49 Grossberg, Nelson and Treichler, *Cultural Studies*; the article in question is Peter Stallybrass, 'Shakespeare, the Individual, and the Text', pp. 593–612.

50 Jean-François Lyotard, *The Postmodern Condition: A Report on Knowledge*, Minneapolis: University of Minnesota Press, 1984.

51 Gianni Vattimo, *The End of Modernity: Nihilism and Hermeneutics in Postmodern Culture*, Baltimore, Johns Hopkins University Press, 1988.

52 Linda Hutcheon. *A Poetics of Postmodernism: History, Theory, Fiction*, New York, Routledge, 1988.

53 Jean Baudrillard, *Simulations*, New York, Semiotext(e), 1983.

54 Jean Baudrillard, *For a Critique of the Political Economy of the Sign*, St. Louis, Telos, 1981.

55 Jean Baudrillard, *The Mirror of Production*, St. Louis, Telos, 1975; *Forget Foucault*, New York, Semiotext(e), 1987.

56 Fredric Jameson, *Postmodernism, or, The Cultural Logic of Late Capitalism*, Durham, North Carolina, Duke University Press, 1991.

57 Donna J. Haraway, *Simians, Cyborgs, and Women: The Reinvention of Nature*, New York, Routledge, 1991, p. 1.

58 *ibid.*, p. 3.

59 *ibid.*, p. 178.

60 *ibid.*, pp. 179–181, 151.

61 See Morag Shiach, *Hélène Cixous: A Politics of Writing*, London, Routledge, 1991, pp. 106–109.

62 Johannes Birringer, *Theatre, Theory, Postmodernism*, Bloomington, Indiana University Press, 1991.

63 *ibid.*, pp. x–xi.

64 *ibid.*, pp. xii–xiii.

65 *ibid.*, p. xiii.

66 *ibid.*, p. 228.

67 Philip Auslander, *Presence and Resistance: Postmodernism and Cultural Politics in Contemporary American Performance*, Ann Arbor, University of Michigan Press, 1992, pp. 4, 7.

68 *ibid.*, p. 4.

69 *ibid.*, p. 81.

70 Tom Stoppard, *The Real Thing*, London, Faber, 1983, p. 25.

71 Alice Rayner, 'Improper Conjunctions: Metaphor, Performance, and Text', *Essays in Theatre* 14.1, November 1995, p. 12.

72 Anna Deavere Smith, *Twilight: Los Angeles, 1992*, New York, Anchor Books, 1994, pp. xxi–xxii.

73 *ibid.*, p. xxiv.

74 *ibid.*, p. 147.

75 *ibid.*, p. 232.

76 *ibid.*, p. xxi.

77 *ibid.*, p. 255.

78 *ibid.*, p. 25.

79 Charles R. Lyons and James Lyons, 'Anna Deavere Smith: Perspectives on her Performance within the Context of Critical Theory', *Journal of Dramatic Theory and Criticism* 9.1, Fall 1994, pp. 62–63.

80 See, for instance, Heiner Müller, 'The Walls of History', *Semiotext(e)* 4.2, 1982, pp. 36–76; '19 Answers by Heiner Müller', *Hamletmachine and Other Texts for the Stage*, New York, Performing Arts Journal Publications, 1984, pp. 137–140.

81 Müller, 'Walls of History', p. 44.

82 Heiner Müller, 'Reflections on Post-Modernism', *New German Critique* 16, Winter 1979, pp. 55–57.

83 Muller, '19 Answers', pp. 137, 140.

84 Müller, *Hamletmachine*, p. 55.

85 *ibid.*, p. 57.

86 Müller, '19 Answers', p. 140.

87 Birringer, *Theatre, Theory, Postmodernism*, p. 62.

88 Carl Weber, 'German Theatre Between The Past and The Future', *Performing Arts Journal* 37, January 1991, p. 48.

89 Margaret Croyden, 'After the Revolution', *The Village Voice*, June 12, 1990, pp. 98, 106.

90 *ibid.*, p. 98.

91 Andreas Höfele, 'A Theater of Exhaustion? 'Posthistoire' in Recent German Shakespeare Productions', *Shakespeare Quarterly* 43.1, Spring 1992, p. 81.

92 *ibid.*, pp. 84, 85.

93 Edward Said, *Orientalism*, New York, Pantheon, 1978.

94 Edward W. Said, *Culture and Imperialism*, New York, Knopf, 1993.

95 *ibid.*, pp. xiii–xiv.

96 Franz Fanon, *The Wretched of the Earth*, London, MacGibbon & Kee, 1965, p. 30.

97 Gayatri Chakravorty Spivak, *In Other Worlds: Essays in Cultural Politics*, New York, Methuen, 1987, p. 92.

98 Gayatri Chakravorty Spivak, 'Can the Subaltern Speak?', *Marxism and the Interpretation of Culture*, eds Cary Nelson and Lawrence Grossberg, Urbana, University of Illinois Press, 1988, p. 286.

99 Homi K. Bhabha, 'The Other Question: Difference, Discrimination and the Discourse of Colonialism', *Literature, Politics and Theory: Papers from the Essex Conference 1976–84*, eds Francis Barker, Peter Hulme, Margaret Iversen and Diana Loxley, London, Methuen, 1986, pp. 148–172.

100 Homi K. Bhabha, 'Postcolonial Authority and Postmodern Guilt', *Cultural Studies*, eds Lawrence Grossberg, Cary Nelson and Paula A. Treichler, New York, Routledge, 1992, pp. 56–68.

101 Trinh T. Minh-Ha, *Framer Framed*, New York, Routledge, 1992, p. 156.

102 Trinh T. Minh-Ha, *Woman, Native, Other: Writing Postcoloniality and Feminism*, Bloomington, Indiana University Press, 1989.

103 For instance, Bill Ashcroft, Gareth Griffiths and Helen Tiffin, eds, *The Post-colonial Studies Reader*, London, Routledge, 1995, and Patrick Williams and Laura Chrisman, eds, *Colonial Discourse and Post-Colonial Theory: A Reader*, New York, Columbia University Press, 1994.

104 Bill Ashcroft, Gareth Griffiths and Helen Tiffin, *The Empire Writes Back: Theory and Practice in Post-Colonial Literatures*, London, Routledge, 1989.

105 Janelle G. Reinelt and Joseph R. Roach, *Critical Theory and Performance*, Ann Arbor, University of Michigan Press, 1992, pp. 9–106. See also J. Ellen Gainor, ed., *Imperialism and Theatre: Essays on World Theatre, Drama and Performance*, London, Routledge, 1995.

106 Terry Goldie, *Fear and Temptation: The Image of the Indigene in Canadian, Australian, and New Zealand Literatures*, Kingston, Ontario, McGill-Queen's University Press, 1989; *Canadian Theatre Review* 74, Spring 1993.

107 Ashcroft, Griffiths and Tiffin, *The Empire Writes Back*, pp. 190–191.

108 Dinesh D'Souza, *Illiberal Education: The Politics of Race and Sex on Campus*, New York, The Free Press, 1991, pp. 70–71.

109 Aimé Césaire, *A Tempest*, New York, Ubu Repertory Theater Publications, 1985.

110 *ibid.*, p. 49.

111 *ibid.*, p. 14.

112 *ibid.*, pp. 43–46.

113 *ibid.*, pp. 52–54.

114 *ibid.*, pp. 23–27, 69–73.

115 *ibid.*, p. 1.

116 David Henry Hwang, *M. Butterfly*, New York, Plume, 1989, p. 95.

117 *ibid.*, p. 95.

118 *ibid.*, p. 91.

119 Tomson Highway, *Dry Lips Oughta Move to Kapuskasing*, Saskatoon, Fifth House, 1989.

120 Tomson Highway, *The Rez Sisters*, Saskatoon, Fifth House, 1988.

121 Alan Filewod, 'Receiving Aboriginality: Tomson Highway and the Crisis of Cultural Authenticity', *Theatre Journal* 46.3, October 1994, pp. 363–373.

122 Ashcroft, Griffiths and Tiffin, *The Empire Writes Back*, pp. 7–8.

123 Highway, *Dry Lips*, p. 12.

124 *ibid.*, pp. 129–130.

125 Paulo Freire, *Pedagogy of the Oppressed*, New York, Seabury, 1970.

126 Abdul R. Janmohamed, 'Some Implications of Paulo Freire's Border Pedagogy', *Between Borders: Pedagogy and the Politics of Cultural Studies*, eds Henry A. Giroux and Peter McLaren, New York, Routledge, 1994, pp. 242–252.

127 Augusto Boal, *Theatre of the Oppressed*, New York, Theatre Communications Group, 1985.

128 *ibid.*, p. 141.

129 *ibid.*, p. 147.

130 *ibid.*, p. 149.

131 *ibid.*, p. 150.

132 *ibid.*, p. 127.

133 *ibid.*, p. 39.

CONCLUSION

1 William Shakespeare, *The Winter's Tale*, *The Riverside Shakespeare*, ed. G. Blakemore Evans, Boston, Houghton-Mifflin, 1974, 5.2.110–111.

2 Ezra Pound, 'Exile's Letter', *Personae*, New York, New Directions, 1971, p. 136.

3 David Lodge, ed., *Modern Criticism and Theory: A Reader*, Longman, London, 1988; Dan Latimer, ed., *Contemporary Critical Theory*, San Diego, Harcourt, 1988; Lawrence Grossberg, Cary Nelson and Paula A. Treichler, eds, *Cultural Studies*, New York, Routledge, 1992.

4 Paul A. Bové, ed., *Early Postmodernism: Foundational Essays*, Durham, North Carolina, Duke University Press, 1995; Joseph Natoli and Linda

Hutcheon, eds, *A Postmodern Reader*, Albany, State University of New York Press, 1993; Bill Ashcroft, Gareth Griffiths and Helen Tiffin, eds, *The Post-colonial Studies Reader*, London, Routledge, 1995; Diana Fuss, ed., *Inside/Out*, New York, Routledge, 1991; Henry Abelove, Michèle Aina Barale and David M. Haplerin, eds, *The Lesbian and Gay Studies Reader*, New York, Routledge, 1993.

5 Fredric Jameson, *The Prison House of Language: A Critical Account of Structuralism and Russian Formalism*, Princeton, Princeton University Press, 1972; Jonathan Culler, *Structuralist Poetics: Structuralism, Linguistics, and the Study of Literature*, Ithaca, Cornell University Press, 1975; Terence Hawkes, *Structuralism and Semiotics*, Berkeley, University of California Press, 1977; Terry Eagleton, *Literary Theory: An Introduction*, Minneapolis, University of Minnesota Press, 1983.

6 Susan Bassnett-McGuire, *Translation Studies*, London, Methuen, 1980; Christopher Norris, *Deconstruction: Theory and Practice*, London, Methuen, 1982; Robert C. Holub, *Reception Theory: A Critical Introduction*, London, Methuen, 1984; Toril Moi, *Sexual/Textual Politics: Feminist Literary Theory*, London, Methuen, 1985.

7 Irena R. Makaryk, ed., *Encyclopedia of Contemporary Literary Theory: Approaches, Scholars, Terms*, Toronto, University of Toronto Press, 1993; Michael Groden and Martin Kreisworth, eds, *The Johns Hopkins Guide to Literary Theory and Criticism*, Baltimore, Johns Hopkins University Press, 1994.

8 Donald G. Marshall, *Contemporary Critical Theory: A Selective Bibliography*, New York, The Modern Language Association of America, 1993.

9 See Peter Brook, *The Empty Space*, New York, Atheneum, 1968.

SELECT BIBLIOGRAPHY

GENERAL

Artaud, Antonin, *The Theater and its Double*, New York, Grove Press, 1958.

——, *Selected Writings*, Berkeley, University of Califomia Press, 1988.

Battcock, Gregory and Robert Nickas, eds, *The Art of Performance: A Critical Anthology*, New York, Dutton, 1984.

Belsey, Catherine, *Critical Practice*, London, Routledge, 1980.

Blau, Herbert, *Blooded Thought: Occasions of Theatre*, New York, Performing Arts Journal Publications, 1982.

——, *Take Up the Bodies: Theater at the Vanishinig Point*, Urbana, University of Illinois Press, 1982.

——, 'Ideology and Performance', *Theatre Journal* 35.4, December 1983, pp. 441–460.

——, 'The Audition of Dream and Events', *Drama Review* 31.3, Fall 1987, pp. 59–73.

——, *The Eye of Prey: Subversions of the Postmodern*, Bloomington, Indiana University Press, 1987.

——, *The Audience*, Baltimore, Johns Hopkins University Press, 1990.

Carlson, Marvin, *Theories of the Theatre: A Historical and Critical Survey from the Greeks to the Present* expanded edition, Ithaca, Cornell University Press, 1993.

——, *Performance: A Critical Introduction*, London, Routledge, 1996.

Culler, Jonathan, *Structuralist Poetics: Structuralism, Linguistics, and the Study of Literature*, Ithaca, Cornell University Press, 1975.

Dukore, Bernard F., *Dramatic Theory and Criticism: Greeks to Grotowski*, New York, Holt, Rinehart, 1974.

Eagleton, Terry, *Literary Theory: An Introduction*, Minneapolis, University of Minnesota Press, 1983.

Easthope, Antony and Kate McGowan, *A Critical and Cultural Theory Reader*, Toronto, University of Toronto Press, 1993.

Fortier, Mark, 'Cultural Studies and Theatre: From Stanislavski to the Vigil', *College Literature* 19.2, June 1992, pp. 91–97.

Groden, Michael and Martin Kreisworth, eds, *The Johns Hopkins Guide to Literary Theory and Criticism*, Baltimore, Johns Hopkins University Press, 1994.

Hawkes, Terence, *Structuralism and Semiotics*, Berkeley, University of California Press, 1977.

Jameson, Fredric, *The Prison House of Language: A Critical Account of Structuralism and Russian Formalism*, Princeton, Princeton University Press, 1972.

Latimer, Dan, ed., *Contemporary Critical Theory*, San Diego, Harcourt, 1988.

Lodge, David, ed., *Modern Criticism and Theory: A Reader*, Longman, London, 1988.

Makaryk, Irena R., ed., *Encyclopedia of Contemporary Literary Theory: Approaches, Scholars, Terms*, Toronto, University of Toronto Press, 1993.

Maranca, Bonnie, 'Theatre and the University at the end of the Twentieth Century', *Performing Arts Journal* 17.2 and 17.3, May/September 1995, pp. 55–71.

Marshall, Donald G., *Contemporary Critical Theory: A Selective Bibliography*, New York, The Modern Language Association of America, 1993.

Pfister, Manfred, *The Theory and Analysis of Drama*, Cambridge, Cambridge University Press, 1991.

Reinelt, Janelle G. and Joseph R. Roach, eds, *Critical Theory and Performance*, Ann Arbor, University of Michigan Press, 1992.

Schechner, Richard, *Performance Theory*, New York, Routledge, 1988.

SEMIOTICS

Barthes, Roland, *Critical Essays*, Evanston, Illinois, Northwestern University Press, 1972.

——, *Mythologies*, London, Jonathan Cape, 1972.

——, *S/Z: An Essay*, New York, Hill & Wang, 1974.

——, *A Lover's Discourse: Fragments*, New York, Hill & Wang, 1978.

——, 'From Work to Text', *Textual-Strategies: Perspectives in Post-Structuralist Criticism*, ed. Josué V. Harari, Ithaca, Cornell University Press, 1979, pp. 73–81.

——, *A Barthes Reader*, ed. Susan Sontag, New York, Hill & Wang, 1982.

——, *The Fashion System*, New York, Hill & Wang, 1983.

——, *The Grain of the Voice: Interviews 1962–1980*, New York, Hill & Wang, 1985.

——, *The Responsibility of Forms: Critical Essays on Music, Art, and Representation*, New York, Hill & Wang, 1985.

——, 'The Death of the Author', *Modern Criticism and Theory*, ed. David Lodge, London, Longman, 1988, pp. 167–172.

Carlson, Marvin, *Theatre Semiotics: Signs of Life*, Bloomington, Indiana University Press, 1990.

Elam, Keir, *The Semiotics of Theatre and Drama*, London, Routledge, 1980.

Pavis, Patrice, 'The Interplay Between Avant-Garde Theatre and Semiology', *Performing Arts Journal* 15, 1981, pp. 75–85.

——, *Languages of the Stage*, New York, PAJ Publications, 1982.

Peirce, Charles, *Peirce on Signs*, ed. James Hoopes, Chapel Hill, University of North Carolina Press, 1991.

Saussure, Ferdinand de, *Course in General Linguistics*, New York, Fontana/Collins, 1974.

Scolnikov, Hanna and Peter Holland, eds, *The Play Out of Context: Transferring Plays from Culture to Culture*, Cambridge, Cambridge University Press, 1987.

PHENOMENOLOGY

Bachelard, Gaston, *The Poetics of Space*, New York, Orion Press, 1964.

Butler, Judith, 'Performative Acts and Gender Constitution: An Essay in Phenomenology and Feminist Theory', *Performing Feminisms: Feminist Critical Theory and Theatre*, ed. Sue-Ellen Case, Baltimore, Johns Hopkins University Press, 1990, pp. 270–282.

Heidegger, Martin, *Poetry, Language, and Truth*, New York, Harper & Row, 1975.

——, *Basic Writings*, New York, Harper & Row, 1977.

——, *The Question Concerning Technology and Other Essays*, New York, Harper & Row, 1977.

Husserl, Edmund, *The Idea of Phenomenology*, The Hague, Martinus Nijhoff, 1964.

Merleau-Ponty, Maurice, *Phenomenology of Perception*, London, Routledge, 1962.

Rayner, Alice, *To Act, To Do, To Perform: Drama and the Phenomenology of Action*, Ann Arbor, University of Michigan Press, 1994.

——, 'Improper Conjunctions: Metaphor, Performance, and Text', *Essays in Theatre* 14.1, November 1995, pp. 3–14.

Sartre, Jean-Paul, *Being and Nothingness: An Essay on Phenomenological Ontology*, New York, Washington Square Press, 1966.

Stanislavski, Constantin, *My Life in Art*, New York, Theatre Arts Books, 1948.

States, Bert O., *Great Reckonings in Little Rooms: On the Phenomenology of Theater*, Berkeley, University of California Press, 1985.

——, 'The Phenomenological Attitude', *Critical Theory and Performance*, eds Janelle G. Reinelt and Joseph R. Roach, Ann Arbor, University of Michigan Press, 1992, pp. 369–379.

Vattimo, Gianni, *The End of Modernity: Nihilism and Hermeneutics in Postmodern Culture*, Baltimore, Johns Hopkins University Press, 1988.

POST-STRUCTURALISM AND DECONSTRUCTION

Constantinidas, Stratos E., *Theatre under Deconstruction: A Question of Approach*, New York, Garland, 1993.

de Man, Paul, *Allegories of Reading: Figural Language in Rousseau, Nietzsche, Rilke, and Proust*, New Haven, Yale University Press, 1979.

——, *The Rhetoric of Romanticism*, New York, Columbia University Press, 1984.

——, *The Resistance to Theory*, Minneapolis, University of Minnesota Press, 1986.

Derrida, Jacques, *Of Grammatology*, Baltimore, Johns Hopkins University Press, 1976.

——, 'Structure, Sign, and Play in the Discourse of the Human Sciences', *Writing and Difference*, Chicago, University of Chicago Press, 1978, pp. 278–293.

——, 'An Interview with Jacques Derrida', James Kearns and Ken Newton, *The Literary Review* 14, April 18–May 1, 1980, pp. 21–22.

——, 'The Law of Genre', *Glyph* 7, Spring 1980, pp. 202–232.

——, *The Ear of the Other: Otobiography, Transference, Translation*, New York, Schocken, 1985.

——, 'But beyond . . . (Open Letter To Anne McClintock and Rob Nixon)', *Critical Inquiry* 13.1, Autumn 1986, pp. 155–170.

——, 'Signature Event Context', *Limited Inc*, Evanston, Illinois, Northwestern University Press, 1988, pp. 1–23.

——, '"Eating Well", or the Calculation of the Subject: An Interview with Jacques Derrida', *Who Comes After the Subject?*, eds Eduardo Cadava, Peter Connor and Jean-Luc Nancy, New York, Routledge, 1991, pp. 96–119.

Fuchs, Elinor, 'Presence and the Revenge of Writing: Re-thinking Theatre After Derrida', *Performing Arts Journal* 26/27, 1985, pp. 163–173.

Grotowski, Jerzy, *Towards a Poor Theatre*, London, Methuen, 1975.

Habermas, Jürgen, *Communication and the Evolution of Society*, London, Heinemann, 1979.

Norris, Christopher, *Deconstruction: Theory and Practice*, London, Methuen, 1982.

Rabkin, Gerald, 'The Play of Misreading: Text/Theatre/Deconstruction', *Performing Arts Journal* 19, 1983, pp. 142–159.

PSYCHOANALYSIS

Alford, Fred C., *The Psychoanalytic Theory of Greek Tragedy*, New Haven, Yale University Press, 1992.

Davis, Walter A., *Get the Guests: Psychoanalysis, Modern American Drama, and the Audience*, Madison, University of Wisconsin Press, 1994.

Deleuze, Gilles, 'Un Manifeste de Moins', *Superpositions*, Carmelo Bene and Gilles Deleuze, Paris, Editions de Minuit, 1979.

——, and Félix Guattari, *Anti-Oedipus*, New York, Viking, 1977.

and ——, *Kafka: Toward a Minor Literature*, Minneapolis, University of Minnesota Press, 1986.

and ——, *A Thousand Plateaus: Capitalism and Schizophrenia*, Minneapolis, University of Minnesota Press, 1987.

Freud, Sigmund, *The Standard Edition of the Complete Psychological Works*, ed. James Strachey, 23 vols, London, Hogarth Press, 1953–1966.

Lacan, Jacques, 'Of Structure as an Imnixing of an Otherness Prerequisite to Any Subject Whatever', *The Languages of Criticism and the Sciences of Man: The Structuralist Controversy*, eds Richard Macksey and Eugenio Donato, Baltimore, Johns Hopkins University Press, 1970, pp. 186–200.

——, 'Seminar on "The Purloined Letter"', *Yale French Studies* 48, 1972, pp. 39–72.

——, 'Desire and the Interpretation of Desire in *Hamlet*', *Yale French Studies* 55/56, 1977, pp. 11–52.

——, *Écrits: A Selection*, New York, Norton, 1977.

——, and the *école freudienne*, *Feminine Sexuality*, eds Juliet Mitchell and Jacqueline Rose, New York, Norton, 1982.

Kowsar, Mohammad, 'Deleuze on Theatre: A Case Study of Carmelo Bene's *Richard III*', *Theatre Journal* 38.1, March 1986, pp. 19–33.

——, 'Lacan's *Antigone*: A Case Study in Psychoanalytic Ethics', *Critical Theory and Performance*, eds Janelle G. Reinelt and Joseph R. Roach, Ann Arbor, University of Michigan Press, 1992, pp. 399–412.

Kristeva, Julia, *Revolution in Poetic Language*, New York, Columbia University Press, 1984.

Landy, Robert J., *Persona and Performance: The Meaning of Role in Drama, Therapy, and Everyday Life*, London, Jessica Kingsley Publishers, 1993.

Žižek, Slavoj, *The Sublime Object of Ideology*, London, Verso, 1989.

——, *Looking Awry: An Introduction to Jacques Lacan through Popular Culture*, Cambridge, Mass., MIT Press, 1991.

——, *Enjoy Your Symptom!: Jacques Lacan in Hollywood and Out*, New York, Routledge, 1992.

FEMINISM AND GENDER THEORY

Abelove, Henry, Michèle Aina Barale and David M. Halperin, eds, *The Lesbian and Gay Studies Reader*, New York, Routledge, 1993.

Aston, Elaine, *An Introduction to Feminism and Theatre*, London, Routledge, 1995.

Austin, Gayle, *Feminist Theories for Dramatic Research*, Ann Arbor, University of Michigan Press, 1990.

Brask, Per, ed., *Essays on Kushner's Angels*, Winnipeg, Blizzard Publishing, 1995.

Butler, Judith, 'Performative Acts and Gender Constitution: An Essay in Phenomenology and Feminist Theory', *Performing Feminisms: Feminist Critical Theory and Theatre*, ed. Sue-Ellen Case, Baltimore, Johns Hopkins University Press, 1990, pp. 270–282.

Carlson, Susan, 'Cannibalizing and Carnivalizing: Reviving Aphra Behn's *The Rover*', *Theatre Journal* 47.4, December 1995, pp. 517–539.

Case, Sue-Ellen, *Feminism and Theatre*, New York, Routledge, 1988.

Christian, Barbra, 'The Race for Theory', *Feminist Studies* 14, Spring 1988, p. 67–79.

Cixous, Hélène, 'Sorties: Out and Out: Attacks/Ways Out/Forays', *The Newly Born Woman*, Hélène Cixous and Catherine Clément, Minneapolis, University of Minnesota Press, 1986, pp. 63–132.

de Lauretis, Teresa, 'Sexual Indifference and Lesbian Representation', Sue-Ellen Case, ed., *Performing Feminisms: Feminist Critical Theory and Theatre*, Baltimore, Johns Hopkins University Press, 1990.

Dolan, Jill, *The Feminist Spectator as Critic*, Ann Arbor, UMI Research Press, 1988.

——, 'Practicing Cultural Disruptions: Gay and Lesbian Representation and Sexuality', *Critical Theory and Performance*, ed. Janelle G. Reinelt and Joseph R. Roach, Ann Arbor, University of Michigan Press, 1992, pp. 263–275.

Foucault, Michel, *The History of Sexuality*, vol. 1, New York, Vintage, 1980.

——, *Power/Knowledge: Selected Interviews and Other Writings 1972–1977*, New York, Pantheon, 1980.

Fuss, Diana, ed., *Inside/Out*, New York, Routledge, 1991.

Garber, Marjorie, *Vested Interests: Cross Dressing and Cultural Anxiety*, New York, Routledge, 1992.

Goldberg, Jonathan, ed., *Queering the Renaissance*, Durham, North Carolina, Duke University Press, 1994.

hooks, bell, 'Representing Whiteness in the Black Imagination', *Cultural Studies*, eds Lawrence Grossberg, Cary Nelson and Paula Treichler, New York, Routledge, 1992, pp. 338–346.

Jones, Heather, 'Feminism and Nationalism in Domestic Melodrama: Gender, Genre, and Canadian Identity', *Essays in Theatre* 8.1, November 1989, pp. 5–14.

Kristeva, Julia, 'Women's Time', *Signs* 7.1, 1981, pp. 13–35.

Lewis, Barbara, 'Back Over the Rainbow', *American Theatre* 12.7, September 1995, p. 6.

McNulty, Charles, 'The Queer as Drama Critic', *Theater* 24.2, 1993, pp. 12–20.

Moi, Toril, *Sexual/Textual Politics: Feminist Literary Theory*, London, Methuen, 1985.

Morton, Donald, 'Birth of the Cyberqueer', *PMLA* 110.3, May 1995, pp. 369–381.

Mulvey, Laura, 'Visual Pleasure and Narrative Cinema', *Screen* 16.3, Autumn 1975, pp. 6–18.

Rich, Adrienne, 'Compulsory Heterosexuality and Lesbian Experience', *Signs* 5, Summer 1980, pp. 631–660.

Russell, Anne, ed., 'Introduction', Aphra Behn, *The Rover or The Banished Cavaliers*, Peterborough, Ontario, Broadview Press, 1994.

Savran, David, 'Ambivalence, Utopia, and a Queer Sort of Materialism: How *Angels in America* Reconstructs the Nation', *Theatre Journal* 47.2, May 1995, pp. 207–227.

Sedgwick, Eve Kosofsky, *The Epistemology of the Closet*, Berkeley, University of California Press, 1990.

Shiach, Morag, *Hélène Cixous: A Politics of Writing*, London, Routledge, 1991, pp. 106–109.

Silverstein, Marc, '"Make Us The Women We Can't Be:" Cloud Nine and The Female Imaginary,' *Journal of Dramatic Theory and Criticism* 8.2, Spring 1994, pp. 7–22.

Wallace, Michelle, 'Negative Images: Towards a Black Feminist Cultural Criticism', *Cultural Studies*, eds Lawrence Grossberg, Cary Nelson and Paula Treichler, New York, Routledge, 1992, pp. 654–671.

Wallace, Robert, 'Towards a Poetics of Gay Male Theatre', *Essays on Canadian Writing* 54, Winter 1994, pp. 212–236.

Wiley, Catherine, review of *for colored girls who have considered suicide when the rainbow is enuf*, *Theatre Journal* 43, 1991, pp. 381–382.

Woolf, Virginia, *A Room of One's Own*, London, Grafton, 1977.

READER-RESPONSE AND RECEPTION THEORY

Barthes, Roland, *S/Z*, New York, Hill & Wang, 1974.

Bassnett-McGuire, Susan, *Translation Studies*, London, Methuen, 1980.

Bennett, Susan, *Theatre Audiences: A Theory of Production and Reception*, London, Routledge, 1990.

Berry, Ralph, *On Directing Shakespeare: Interviews with Contemporary Directors*, London, Croom Helm, 1977.

Brook, Peter, *The Empty Space*, New York, Atheneum, 1968.

——, *The Shifting Point*, New York, Harper & Row, 1987.

Carlson, Marvin, *Theatre Semiotics: Signs of Life*, Bloomington, Indiana University Press, 1990.

Derrida, Jacques, 'Des Tours de Babel', *Difference in Translation*, ed. Joseph F. Graham, Ithaca, Cornell University Press, 1985, pp. 165–207.

——, *The Ear of the Other: Otobiography, Transference, Translation*, New York, Schocken, 1985, pp. 157–158.

Fish, Stanley, *Is There a Text in This Class? The Authority of Interpretive Communities*, Cambridge, Mass., Harvard University Press, 1980.

Hermans, Theo, ed., *The Manipulation of Literature: Studies in Literary Translation*, London, Croom Helm, 1983.

Holub, Robert C. *Reception Theory: A Critical Introduction*, London, Methuen, 1984.

Iser, Wolfgang, *The Act of Reading: A Theory of Aesthetic Response*, Baltimore, Johns Hopkins University Press, 1978.

Jauss, Hans Robert, *Toward an Aesthetic of Reception*, Minneapolis, University of Minnesota Press, 1982.

Loney, Glenn, ed., *Peter Brook's Production of Shakespeare's* A Midsummer

Night's Dream *for the Royal Shakespeare Company: The Complete and Authorized Acting Edition*, Stratford, Royal Shakespeare Company, 1974.

Mufson, Daniel, 'Sexual Perversity in Viragos', *Theater* 24.1, 1993, pp. 111–113.

Rabkin, Gerald, 'Is There a Text On This Stage: Theatre/Authorship/Interpretation', *Performing Arts Journal* 26/27, 1985, pp. 142–159.

Selbourne, David, *The Making of A MIDSUMMER NIGHT'S DREAM: An Eye-witness Account of Peter Brook's Production from First Rehearsal to Opening Night*, London, Methuen, 1982.

MATERIALISM

Adorno, Theodor, *Aesthetic Theory*, London, Routledge, 1984.

Althusser, Louis, *For Marx*, London, Verso, 1969.

——, 'Ideology and Ideological State Apparatuses (Notes towards an Investigation)', *Lenin and Philosophy and other essays*, London, NLB, 1971, pp. 123–173.

Benjamin, Walter, *Illuminations*, New York, Schocken, 1969.

——, *The Origin of German Tragic Drama*, London, NLB, 1977.

Bennett, Tony, *Formalism and Marxism*, London, Methuen, 1977.

Brecht, Bertolt, *Brecht on Theatre*, New York, Hill & Wang, 1964.

Cohen, Walter, *Drama of a Nation: Public Theater in Renaissance England and Spain*, Ithaca, Cornell University Press, 1985.

Davies, Ioan, *Cultural Studies and Beyond: Fragments of Empire*, London, Routledge, 1995.

Dollimore, Jonathan, *Radical Tragedy: Religion, Ideology and Power in the Drama of Shakespeare and his Contemporaries*, Chicago, University of Chicago Press, 1984.

——, and Alan Sinfield, eds, *Political Shakespeare: New Essays in Cultural Materialism*, Ithaca, Cornell University Press, 1985.

Eagleton, Terry, *Walter Benjamin or Towards a Revolutionary Criticism*, London, Verso, 1981.

——, *Ideology: An Introduction*, London, Verso, 1991.

Feltes, N. N., *Modes of Production of Victorian Novels*, Chicago, University of Chicago Press, 1986.

Foucault, Michel, *The Order of Things: An Archeology of the Human Sciences*, New York, Vintage, 1973.

——, *Language, Counter-Memory, Practice: Selected Essays and Interviews*, Ithaca, Cornell University Press, 1977.

——, *The History of Sexuality*, vol. 1, New York, Vintage, 1980.

——, *Power/Knowledge: Selected Interviews and Other Writings 1972–1977*, New York, Pantheon, 1980.

——, 'Of Other Spaces', *Diacritics* 16.1, Spring 1986, pp. 24–27.

Greenblatt, Stephen, *Shakespearean Negotiations: The Circulation of Social Energy in Renaissance England*, Berkeley, University of California Press, 1988.

Grossberg, Lawrence, Cary Nelson and Paula Treichler, eds, 'Cultural Studies: An Introduction', *Cultural Studies*, New York, Routledge, 1992.

Gurr, Andrew, *Playgoing in Shakespeare's London*, Cambridge, Cambridge University Press, 1987.

Holderness, Graham, ed., *The Shakespeare Myth*, Manchester, Manchester University Press, 1988.

Jameson, Fredric, *The Political Unconscious: Narrative as a Socially Symbolic Act*, Ithaca, Cornell University Press, 1981.

Knowles, Richard Paul, 'From Nationalist to Multinational: The Stratford Festival, Free Trade, and the Discourses of Intercultural Tourism,' unpublished paper, 1994.

——, 'Shakespeare, 1993, and the Discourses of the Stratford Festival, Ontario', *Shakespeare Quarterly* 45.2, Summer 1994, pp. 211–225.

Macherey, Pierre, *A Theory of Literary Production*, London, Routledge, 1978.

Marx, Karl, *Economic and Philosophic Manuscripts of 1844*, New York, International, 1964.

——, *Capital*, vol. 1, New York, Vintage, 1977.

Smith, Gary, ed., *Benjamin: Philosophy, History, Aesthetics*, Chicago, University of Chicago Press, 1989.

Smith, Paul, *Discerning the Subject*, Minneapolis, University of Minnesota Press, 1988.

Taylor, Gary, *Reinventing Shakespeare: A Cultural History from the Restoration to the Present*, New York, Weidenfeld & Nicolson, 1989.

Wallace, Robert, *Producing Marginality: Theatre and Criticism in Canada*, Saskatoon, Fifth House, 1990.

Williams, Raymond, *Marxism and Literature*, Oxford, Oxford University Press, 1977.

——, *Towards 2000*, London, Chatto & Windus, 1983.

POSTMODERNISM

Auslander, Philip, *Presence and Resistance: Postmodernism and Cultural Politics in Contemporary American Performance*, Ann Arbor, University of Michigan Press, 1992.

Baudrillard, Jean, *The Mirror of Production*, St. Louis, Telos, 1975.

——, *For a Critique of the Political Economy of the Sign*, St. Louis, Telos, 1981.

——, *Simulations*, New York, Semiotext(e), 1983.

——, *Forget Foucault*, New York, Semiotext(e), 1987.

Birringer, Johannes, *Theatre, Theory, Postmodernism*, Bloomington, Indiana University Press, 1991.

Bové, Paul A., ed., *Early Postmodernism: Foundational Essays*, Durham, North Carolina, Duke University Press, 1995.

Haraway, Donna J., *Simians, Cyborgs, and Women: The Reinvention of Nature*, New York, Routledge, 1991.

Höfele, Andreas, 'A Theater of Exhaustion? "Posthistoire" in Recent German Shakespeare Productions', *Shakespeare Quarterly* 43.1, Spring 1992, pp. 80–86.

Hutcheon, Linda, *A Poetics of Postmodernism: History, Theory, Fiction*, New York, Routledge, 1988.

Jameson, Fredric, *Postmodernism, or, The Cultural Logic of Late Capitalism*, Durham, North Carolina, Duke University Press, 1991.

Lyons, Charles R. and James Lyons, 'Anna Deavere Smith: Perspectives on her Performance within the Context of Critical Theory', *Journal of Dramatic Theory and Criticism* 9.1, Fall 1994, pp. 43–66.

Lyotard, Jean-François, *The Postmodern Condition: A Report on Knowledge*, Minneapolis, University of Minnesota Press, 1984.

Müller, Heiner, 'Reflections on Post-Modernism', *New German Critique* 16, Winter 1979, pp. 55–57.

——, 'The Walls of History', *Semiotext(e)* 4.2, 1982, pp. 36–76.

Natoli, Joseph and Linda Hutcheon, eds, *A Postmodern Reader*, Albany, State University of New York Press, 1993.

Ross, Andrew, ed., *Universal Abandon? The Politics of Postmodernism*, Minneapolis, University of Minnesota Press, 1988.

Vattimo, Gianni, *The End of Modernity: Nihilism and Hermeneutics in Postmodern Culture*, Baltimore, Johns Hopkins University Press, 1988.

Weber, Carl, 'German Theatre Between The Past and The Future', *Performing Arts Journal* 37, January 1991, pp. 43–59.

POST-COLONIALISM

Ashcroft, Bill, Gareth Griffiths and Helen Tiffin, *The Empire Writes Back: Theory and Practice in Post-Colonial Literatures*, London, Routledge, 1989.

——, eds, *The Post-colonial Studies Reader*, London, Routledge, 1995.

Bhabha, Homi K., 'The Other Question: Difference, Discrimination and the Discourse of Colonialism', *Literature, Politics and Theory: Papers from the Essex Conference 1976–84*, eds Francis Barker, Peter Hulme, Margaret Iversen and Diana Loxley, London, Methuen, 1986, pp. 148–172.

——, 'Postcolonial Authority and Postmodern Guilt', *Cultural Studies*, eds Lawrence Grossberg, Cary Nelson and Paula A. Treichler, New York, Routledge, 1992, pp. 56–68.

Boal, Augusto, *Theatre of the Oppressed*, New York, Theatre Communications Group, 1985.

Fanon, Franz, *The Wretched of the Earth*, London, MacGibbon & Kee, 1965.

Filewod, Alan, 'Receiving Aboriginality: Tomson Highway and the Crisis of Cultural Authenticity', *Theatre Journal* 46.3, October 1994, pp. 363–373.

Freire, Paulo, *Pedagogy of the Oppressed*, New York, Seabury, 1970.

——, *Pedagogy of Hope: Reliving Pedagogy of the Oppressed*, New York, Continuum, 1994.

Gainor, J. Ellen, ed., *Imperialism and Theatre: Essays on World Theatre, Drama and Performance*, London, Routledge, 1995.

Gilbert, Helen and Joanne Tompkins, *Post-Colonial Drama: Theory, Practice, Politics*, London, Routledge, 1996.

Goldie, Terry, *Fear and Temptation: The Image of the Indigene in Canadian, Australian, and New Zealand Literatures*, Kingston, Ontario, McGill-Queen's University Press, 1989.

Janmohamed, Abdul R., 'Some Implications of Paulo Freire's Border Pedagogy', *Between Borders: Pedagogy and the Politics of Cultural Studies*, eds Henry A. Giroux and Peter McLaren, New York, Routledge, 1994, pp. 242–252.

McLaren, Peter and Peter Leonard, eds, *Paulo Freire: A Critical Encounter*, London, Routledge, 1993.

Minh-Ha, Trinh T., *Woman, Native, Other: Writing Postcoloniality and Feminism*, Bloomington, Indiana University Press, 1989.

——, *Framer Framed*, New York, Routledge, 1992.

Said, Edward, *Orientalism*, New York, Pantheon, 1978.

——, *Culture and Imperialism*, New York, Knopf, 1993.

Spivak, Gayatri Chakravorty, *In Other Worlds: Essays in Cultural Politics*, New York, Methuen, 1987.

——, 'Can the Subaltern Speak?', *Marxism and the Interpretation of Culture*, eds Cary Nelson and Lawrence Grossberg, Urbana, University of Illinois Press, 1988, pp. 271–313.

Williams, Patrick and Laura Chrisman, eds, *Colonial Discourse and Post-Colonial Theory: A Reader*, New York, Columbia University Press, 1994.

INDEX

action: in the theatre 31
actor(s) 32, 41, 52, 100; and author
    63, 64, 94; boy actors in
    Renaissance theatre 84; and
    character(s) 25, 65, 78; and
    reception in theatre 54, 98; role
    of 25, 64
adaptation: of earlier works 90,
    91
Adorno, Theodor 40, 105
agent/agency: meaning of the term
    53; women as 73
Akalaitis, JoAnne 74
Akropolis see Grotowski
allegory 26, 90
Althusser, Louis 53, 104, 105, 107
American Repertory Company 91
Angels in America see Kushner
Antigone see Sophocles
apparatuses: in Foucault 107, 112
Artaud, Antonin 5, 7, 12, 42–7, 51,
    59, 111, 143
As You Like It see Shakespeare
Ashcroft, Bill 132, 133, 138
Aston, Elain 70
audience: female 72; response of
    54, 91, 92, 93–4, 98; role of 27,
    53, 67, 100, 140–1; in
    Shakespeare 28, 110; *see also*
    reader-response/reception
    theory
Auslander, Philip 122–3
Austin, Gayle 8, 70
author: authorial control 41, 65;
    and character 63, 64; death of
    21, 63; and director 92, 94, 95–7,

100; in drama/theatre 52, 65, 91,
    92; and reader 54, 89

Bacchae, The see Euripides
Bachelard, Gaston 29
Bakhtin, Mikhail 2
Barrault, Jean-Louis 45
Barthes, Roland 7, 20–1, 37, 41, 88,
    91; on Brecht 23–7
Barton, John 74
Bassnett-McGuire, Susan 146
Baudrillard, Jean 8, 118, 119, 121
Beauty and the Beast (Disney
    production) 108
Beauvoir, Simone de 2
Beck, Julian 32
Beckett, Samuel: *Endgame* 91
Behn, Aphra 74
Being: in Vattimo 31
Belsey, Catherine 7
Bene, Carmelo 65–6
Benjamin, Walter 2, 8, 26, 86, 106,
    109, 113, 131, 136
Benmussa, Simone 69
Bennett, Susan 91
Bennett, Tony 88
Bernhard, Sandra 122
Bhabha, Homi 132, 136
Birringer, Johannes 121–2, 128
black feminism *see* feminist theory:
    black feminism
Blau, Herbert 8, 9, 12, 13, 65, 66,
    67, 68, 128, 143; *Crooked Eclipses*
    48, 49, 90; and deconstruction
    48–9; *Elsinore* 48, 49, 90
Boal, Augusto 12, 140–2, 143;